DESIGNED

up

A designer's
guide on how to
lead inside the
tech industry

DESIGNED

up

A designer's guide on how to
lead inside the tech industry

EMMA CARTER

CRC Press
Taylor & Francis Group

AN AUERBACH BOOK

First edition published 2023
by CRC Press
6000 Broken Sound Parkway NW, Suite 300, Boca Raton, FL 33487-2742
and by CRC Press
2 Park Square, Milton Park, Abingdon, Oxon, OX14 4RN

Library of Congress Cataloging-in-Publication Data
A catalog record has been requested for this title.

ISBN: (hbk) 9781032362144
ISBN: (pbk) 9781032202013
ISBN: (ebk) 9781003330783
DOI: 10.1201/9781003330783

Typeset in Montserrat
by DerryField Publishing Services

trademarks used in this book

for

Mark, and the 24 years of support, laughter and the many, many adventures; for your honesty—and the funny faces you pull when I'm trying to concentrate on writing.

Dearest James, my little problem solver; at the tender age of 6, when I tell you we 'can't' do something, you always have several practical solutions to the problem. Never lose your enthusiasm for learning and problem solving.

Little Harriet, my almost 4 year-old luminary who loves to experiment and see what is possible. Never lose your wild and extraordinary imagination.

I love you more than chocolate cake with sprinkles on top and love hearts.

contents

illustrations and images

Foreword

there has never been a better time to embark on a career in design. Designers are in high demand, and there are countless potential career paths. Design is required for almost every industry, and there is a growing number of design specialisations. I have been fortunate to experience some of these, including publishing, advertising, marketing, branding, packaging, signage, multimedia and digital. I've seen society's expectations of designers change as, increasingly, designers become technologists. The path of innovation and creativity is enabled by new and rapidly evolving technologies which, in the hands of talented designers, can solve our most urgent problems. But to deliver true innovation, designers must be accomplished researchers, good consultants, effective communicators and trusted collaborators. Designers walk the line between art and science, as they create new experiences that deliver measurable value to consumers.

Emma Carter is well travelled when it comes to design paths, having herself led the design of products and brands crossing many mediums and domains. During her career, she has seen entire new frontiers of design and technology open up as digital has taken off and created new opportunities for innovation. This book is the result of extensive research with designers and business leaders across the globe and across different industries.

DesignedUp offers readers many insights into the central role of design in organisations today. Increasingly design is recognised as being indispensable to the creation of competitive advantage, and this realisation is driving the ongoing acquisition of design agencies by large consultancies, tech giants and businesses across the globe.

The opportunities for designers to pick meaningful career paths have broadened. Navigating the many options can be daunting, but *DesignedUp* can help designers understand the differences between working with a technology firm, a consultancy, an agency or a product company. Emma has also run her own agency, and she understands the challenge of going out on one's own and building a brand and a business from nothing.

Many designers allow their careers to be shaped by happenstance and circumstances seemingly outside of their control. This is true of much of my own career. Whilst I made some deliberate choices like moving into digital after a career in print, I also found myself in the situation of working for a small agency that was acquired by a big global consulting firm.

I wish I had known then what to expect, but this was in the early days of digital, before the .com crash of 2000. In the leadup to the acquisition, there was much nervous trepidation amongst our team of designers and developers. The acquiring company did little to set our minds at ease, sending us their *'Dressed to Win'* clothing policy as we prepared for our physical relocation to their shiny CBD office tower.

Amongst the corporate Country Road suits and twinsets in that humourless policy, there was a section titled 'What NOT to wear', which resembled most of my 90s grunge wardrobe. I also suffered the existential discomfort of knowing that my new employer had not chosen me, but rather had chosen the agency I worked for. I probably came across as a dubious denim-clad introvert with a portfolio that they had never seen. They had no idea about my skills and experience as a designer.

Since then, I have learnt to communicate the value of design and promote my own capabilities to my colleagues, clients and leadership, but self-promotion does not come naturally to many.

For designers to be effective in large consulting and technology firms, they need to work on their influence. They need to communicate the value of their work and talk about their process. This is particularly true for designers in creative agencies that get acquired by larger firms looking to increase their design capability.

From my own experience working in both global consulting and technology firms, leaders often have a very narrow understanding of the role of design. Design is often reduced to an aesthetic capability focused upon the form rather than the function of a product or service.

Designers know that form follows function. Many leadership teams fail to recognise the real opportunities presented by skilled designers—to solve

> **Designers need to communicate the value of their work and talk about their process.**

problems and create novel solutions, tested and validated by end users. This is the real work of the designer, regardless of their chosen field of specialisation, and it can't happen from within an ivory tower. Designers who can clearly articulate their value and their process are the ones that will succeed in large technology firms. To achieve this, designers need to design in the open, collaborating with their teams, stakeholders and technologists.

Designers who can make their process visible and invite others in to participate will be better understood, respected and listened to. In my work, this involves pairing with software engineers, sketching ideas with end users and sharing the failures and successes with stakeholders. I have often seen siloed UX teams fail within large organisations because the designers weren't visible to the business and they weren't working in agile lockstep with delivery teams.

In contrast to many large technology firms, my own employer, Thoughtworks®, has taken a different approach to building our design capabilities, primarily through organic growth. We have recruited designers from across the world, evaluating them on more than just their portfolio, seeking to identify like-minded collaborators who understand agile ways of working and are willing to embed themselves inside delivery teams, solving customer challenges as a team.

However, as we have grown and become a public company, this strategy is starting to change, and we have indeed acquired agencies with talented designers. However, our due diligence is focused on alignment on our ways of working to ensure we continue to empower designers and provide environments where they can have a positive impact.

For design leaders, there is much we can do to ensure we support designers early in their careers. For designers to succeed within large organisations, they need guidance and strategies to improve their influence, first within their teams and then beyond, within their organisations and within their local communities.

When working with large, distributed teams, it is important to share our design principles and common ways of working, provide frameworks for mentoring and pairing, and ensure that good platforms exist to encourage community building and knowledge sharing. This has never been more important as we are increasingly working from home after the pandemic changed our working lives forever.

For designers to be effective, they need the right tools and practices to connect with their users, their stakeholders and teams. I believe that *DesignedUp* will help readers to understand how designers can have both a positive influence within the organisation and a genuine impact in the world.

Kate Linton
Head of Design, Thoughtworks

We call someone a leader not because they are in charge but because they have the courage to go first. To risk first. To trust first. First into the unknown.

Sinek

ittle
note

You might be wondering not only 'how did we get here?', but also how I got to this point in my career. Why should I, of all people, be giving advice on how to become 'DesignedUp', and what on earth do I know about being a designer in the tech consulting world?

I always knew a creative path was for me. Growing up in the UK enabled me to experience a vast array of design disciplines from a young age; my mum took me to specialist art classes after school when I was 10 years old, and the secondary school I attended enabled me to take separate subjects in fine art, graphic design, 3D and woodwork, opening my world to endless possibilities and enabling me to take a different lens to solve each problem.

My passion for design and solving problems took me down the graphic design path; however, I knew the world at the time was changing, and the future was heading towards a more digital world. This set the path for my choice in design degree that covered both digital and traditional forms of graphic design, with a strong focus on the fundamentals and foundations of design. Being curious about design, technology, the user and what the future would hold set the direction for my final major degree project. I guesstimated what the future would be like in 15 years' time and designed solutions that would bring together design, usability and technology to enhance users' lives. Fast-forward to today—it's interesting to see how some of my predictions came true and are used by millions every day, such as smart watches, speech to text and speech translation into other languages, showing how our tiny devices enable us to control our smart home when we're miles away. If only I'd had the foresight to go ahead and make them a reality back then!

At 25 I was spending my time travelling between France and London. It was during this transient time that I founded a design agency, which later become an award winner. We focused on the total brand experience, bringing branding, traditional and digital design together to ensure the brand purpose and customer experience were considered at every touchpoint. Clients included renowned retail brand Jack Wills®; Simon Dixon, CEO and co-founder of BnkToTheFuture, now the largest global online investment platform, investing in FinTech, blockchain and bitcoin companies; Steve Bolton, founder of the largest property franchise in the UK; and Mike Harris, founding CEO of Firstdirect, CEO of Mercury Communications®, founding CEO of Egg Banking plc and co-founder of semantic web company Garlik®.

Simon, Steve and Mike became trusted mentors, and Simon and his wife Bliss's encouragement resulted in the successful launch of my first book, *Beyond the Logo,*[*]

---

[*] Carter, E. (2013). *Beyond the Logo.* Beyond Creative Thinking. ISBN-13: 978-0957521407.

which became a best seller on Amazon®. Wanting to add that extra element and mix traditional design with future tech, the book uses augmented reality (AR) to bring its contents to life. It's the first branding and design book to use AR.

My career and life then moved halfway round the world to Australia, where my husband and I decided to embark on a new adventure 'down under'. It was then that I decided to try life on the other side of the fence after being approached by Thoughtworks®, a global tech consultancy, to bring my design knowledge into the world of tech consulting. My career went from a design agency, where I focused solely on managing client expectations, to include navigating the world of agile development as a minority among tech consultants—some of whom didn't quite understand the value of design or hadn't worked with a designer before. Like technology, the organisation is forever changing and adapting to become a better version of itself, and Thoughtworks is now seen as a leading global technology consultancy that integrates strategy, design and software engineering. I'm now a Principal Experience Designer and part of the global design leadership team at Thoughtworks.

Having run an agency and worked in a technology consultancy, I've seen how models operate and know the different skills and mindset required from a designer in each. Yes, there are similarities, but consultants need to show more than just good *design* skills; they need good *consulting* skills and the ability to think quickly for themselves, confidently helping their clients to understand the reason for their choice of direction, design and risks. More than that, design leaders in a tech consultancy need to be true ambassadors of design, understand technology constraints and business needs and steer organisations towards understanding and valuing design, embedding it into every delivery team.

Throughout my career, I've been approached by many designers wanting to know how they can take the lead for themselves. And so—through a series of interviews conducted with various designers and design leaders in the consulting world—I've gathered together insights and experience, including my own, to show what it really takes to go from designer to design leader in a tech consultancy.

As you embark on your own journey to becoming DesignedUp, I'd love to hear about your successes, challenges and failures—the more we share, the more we can learn. Please feel free to get in touch with me on LinkedIn® at https://www.linkedin.com/in/emmacartersealey/

Enjoy the journey!

int

tro.

We've seen a number of consultancies acquiring design agencies in recent years in a bid to fast-track their design capabilities. While many designers have been navigating these new and different worlds, some have chosen to leave the design agency world and independently join tech and business consultancies. In this Introduction you'll gain an understanding of how consultancies are growing their design capabilities, how to lead as a designer inside a large tech consultancy and, through real-life examples, see how a traditional design company has adopted the use of AR and VR to revolutionise how they work and avoid losing their jobs to cheaper overseas providers.

the design career path was once agency focused. You would join as a junior and work your way up to Art or Creative Director and so on. When I started my career, most agencies focused on one area—web design, advertising, print, branding, etc. Few had started to make the shift into multi-disciplinary agencies.

Digital agencies would work in what we now refer to as 'waterfall', where designers do their thing and then hand over to the development team. I was fortunate enough to start out working alongside developers; therefore, I've always been used to collaborating to ensure the experience is the best it can be through pushing the expectations of technology.

The moving tide of change

Since 2004, over one hundred design-related companies have been acquired, over sixty percent of them since 2015.

John Maeda, 2019 Design in Tech Report
Technology x Business x Design

Because of the many acquisitions and companies that embrace design thinking without really knowing what it really means or entails, designers have been left in a position where they are having to navigate a new world of tech and business while explaining what design is and how it should work in this new world. Designers, especially those in the consulting world, can no longer just design; they need to be consultants first and designers second and lead their teams and clients to understand the nuances of design.

Technology plays a huge role in our lives today, and this isn't going to slow down. Our expectations as users constantly demand more from the experience we have when using technology—we expect it to make our jobs and lives increasingly easier. We no longer want to just track our fitness and buy a new pair of trainers when the soles wear out; we want our trainers to tell us when we need an upgrade and what type of shoe best suits our feet for performance. We no longer want to wait for public transport that's rarely on time; we want the convenience of hopping on a scooter or getting the nearest rideshare. We can no longer wait a few days for an online order to arrive; we want it to arrive the same day. We want convenience and we want it now!

And we fully expect the same conveniences that we enjoy in our everyday lives to be replicated in the software and technology we use at work. Unfortunately, the majority of organisations find it hard to improve internal software systems due to costs, legacy technical infrastructure, many systems not being built to 'talk to one another' and so on. This is gradually changing but is going to take longer than the prioritised consumer-facing technology.

However, it's vital that organisations focus on improving these internal systems because of the hugely positive impact the increased efficiency will have on their bottom line. Mundane tasks can be automated, leaving staff time to work on more valuable jobs, and the time it takes to complete jobs can be reduced, leading to more work being won. Staff, no longer bogged down by repetitive, low-value tasks, will experience increased job satisfaction, which can lead to their being even more efficient and productive.

Solving these internal system issues and meeting the ever-increasing expectations of staff can't be achieved with technology alone—it requires the help of designers to fully understand the problem, empathise with users, design better solutions and test them properly.

The technology industry itself is also changing to meet business and customer demands and adopt better delivery practices. Using agile (or a form of agile) to deliver software and digital products is now commonplace. It enables companies to deliver faster to customers, test ideas and get feedback so they can constantly improve through technology advances and stay ahead of customer expectations. For example, Etsy® deploys code 50 times a day to its production servers and now has fewer disruptions than when the company used a waterfall approach. Amazon® engineers deploy code every 11.7 seconds on average, reducing the number and duration of outages while increasing revenue. And Netflix® engineers deploy code thousands of times a day.

These deployments span a whole host of improvements. Some will be 'tech debt' to improve the internal quality of the system, and although this doesn't directly affect the user, it does affect the ability of the team to make changes at speed, which will eventually have an impact on the user experience. There will also be a whole host of new features, bug fixes, UX/ UI improvements and a lot of A/B testing. Some of the periodical bigger changes will be obvious to users, but if you look closely enough at Netflix, for instance, you'll see minor changes happening all the time.

Adopting this approach of continuous design and delivery shows how quickly we can get an idea out into the world and get customer feedback to help drive the perpetual loop.

UAP: Technology, design and art working in harmony

Urban Art Projects (UAP) collaborates with emerging and established artists, architects, developers and designers to build art and installations for the public realm. Their projects include **Florentijn Hofman's 'Kraken'** in Shenzhen, China, and the **J. Mayer H. and Partners 'XXX Times Square with Love'** (starting on page 10) in New York City.

A few years ago, they started looking at how they could use technology to improve on their traditional ways of working—how it could take away some of the less interesting parts of their jobs, improve their processes and help them create more accurate designs—and it's had a huge impact. For instance, by introducing augmented reality (AR) and virtual reality (VR), their designers are now able to take an artist's model, upscale it, use VR to build and manipulate the design and then use AR with Google® Glass® to shortcut some of the tedious planning processes and enable craftsmen to get to the build stage much faster.

One of the first robotic applications they tested was using a robotic arm to mill sand moulds for the production of **Emily Floyd's 'Poll'** (starting on page 14), the first of an edition of five sculptural parrots. Milling the moulds bypassed the need to create physical patterns to form sand moulds (the traditional approach for sand casting), allowing the sculpting to take place in a virtual reality environment. Through robotics, UAP was also able to build a system for linishing stainless steel panels—a finishing technique that smooths and polishes—which enabled them to create a work for artist **Lindy Lee, 'The Ripples of 1,000 Elemental Affirmations'** (see page 16)—the only supplier in Australia that could provide this service.

In an interview with UAP, I asked Gilbert Guaring, Head of Marketing & Communications, how the evolution and expansion happened.

> UAP's creative process and the wide range of projects we deliver have been instrumental in our engagement with technological experimentation. The range of project types mean that, day to day, we have a lot of problem-solving challenges. This relationship and frequency of problem solving makes it easier to test something new, even if we do have a

Florentijn Hofman, Kraken 2017. Images courtesy of the artist and UAP | Urban Art Projects. Photography by Charlie Xia. (Right and next page.)

backup methodology. In addition to that, we have a courageous and talented team and a culture instilled by Matthew and Daniel Tobin's fearless approach to trying something new.

The most important aspect of this process is leveraging our team's wealth of experience and knowledge of traditional methods and incorporating those learnings into the use of emerging digital tools. We believe we are building new career paths for our people and, in doing so, preserving traditional craft and knowledge as well as engaging with the new. For instance, we're using AR technology to bypass the need to create onerous amounts of 2D drawings to communicate a 3D form/3D CAD model. Instead, our workshop team can clip a HoloLense onto a hard hat and look at an accurate holographic image of what they're building, tethered to the actual location on the shop floor where it will be created. This method provides the same detail as those archaic 2D drawings, but it's easier to read and interpret, and the efficiency gains for us have been remarkable.

[Text continues on page 14]

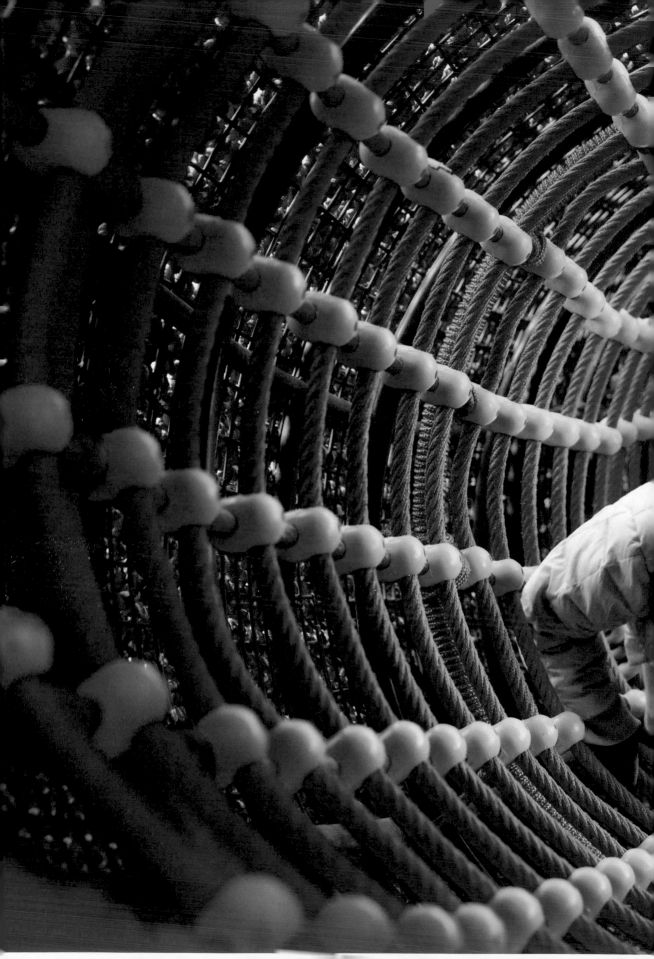

J. Mayer H. and Partners, XXX Times Square with Love 2016.
Images courtesy of the artist and Time Square Arts. (This and next page.)

And, of course, UAP has been using wireless VR systems to create walkable immersive spaces to showcase concepts to clients and artists. We have

Robot creating the model. Emily Floyd, 'Poll' 2017. Images courtesy of the artist and UAP | Urban Art Projects. Photography by Rachel See. (Below and next page.)

been able to reduce projects from eight days down to three, which also reduces cost. These tools are simplifying and enriching the way we work, letting people focus on their craft and the most rewarding parts of their work.

[Text continues on page 18]

Lindy Lee, 'The Ripples of 1,000
Elemental Affirmations' 2019.
Images courtesy of the artist
and UAP | Urban Art Projects.
Photography by Rachel See.

Partner Ben Tait says a new world has unfolded at UAP. In the past, the design team would translate and communicate the artist's agenda to the manufacturing floor. Today, the new team are cross-reality designers, who program machines, working from a creative starting point.

> On the workshop floor we are discovering that, for example, a welder does one thing whereas the robot is capable of a huge range of processes. That's how the new technology differs from its predecessors. Artists approach us with a wide range of creative drivers, and we can match them nicely with a human team in the middle.

And technologies such as VR and AR reduce waste, empower design and allow shorter delivery times. Ben continues:

> This marks a different role for the designer, but the process that follows is the same. Like any tool, robots don't behave exactly as you imagine they will, and the whole team is involved in fine-tuning equipment, with these learnings then applied to the next project. What has been a surprise for UAP is that we are employing more people. In our world, robots mean more jobs rather than fewer.

Combining technology and art has enabled UAP not only to advance their processes and employ more people while also keeping its business in Australia. Founder Matt Tobin finds:

> Ten years ago, we thought our workshop in Australia would be a prototype workshop and everything would be made in China. A decade on, we know that is entirely inaccurate. To be viable and competitive as a manufacturer, especially as a custom manufacturer, it's going to be cheaper to do it locally.

UAP workshop team work with a holographic image of what they're building, tethered to the actual location on the shop floor where it will be created. (This piage and next. Images used with permission of UAP)

Worlds collide

With technology playing such a large part in our everyday lives, these advances have allowed us to turn perceived 'futuristic' ideas into reality and deliver them into the hands of everyday people. Tesla®, AR, VR, Uber® and Lime® scooters have all changed the shape of how we act as humans. It's now OK to get into a stranger's car! And the resulting rise of the 'share economy' has created multibillion-dollar opportunities for businesses.

Mobile AR has been proven to result in more 'mindshare' and has enabled brands including Nestle® and Gucci® to create richer and more emotional experiences to communicate their brand with younger consumers. Danone® seized the opportunity to engage with younger consumers in Belarus and Russia by giving them a unique experience to learn English. They used AR to bring a series of 3D characters to life on magnets to teach kids English words—helping increase their sales of kids' yoghurts while filling a gap in education. Danone found that while there's no immediate way to convert interest to sales, it's said that two-thirds of customers' decisions are based on the quality of their experience with a brand or product.

The advances of AR and VR will undoubtedly see the rise of spatial communications in the future, but ensuring that these are great experiences for consumers can only be achieved through strong collaboration between design and technology.

The sudden shift of organisations adopting remote working due to COVID-19—and many liking the 'new normal'—has resulted in a surge in demand for software advances and better user experiences. Consumers' habits have changed, and their increased adoption of online purchasing quickly highlighted the gaps in technology within those companies that couldn't scale and adapt quickly enough to cope with the sudden surge in transactions. While many businesses have failed during this period, others have successfully taken the opportunity to develop technologies that meet the demands of this 'new' consumer and enable those in remote locations to continue working.

This expansion of technology across all touch-points can only be achieved effectively through the collaboration of design and technology. Design for design's sake doesn't work. For it to truly change an organisation, it has to be baked into the core, integrated across departments and included in every decision the product teams make. Design and tech need to sit side by side at the heart of the organisation, and designers need to be embedded into delivery teams.

The technology industry, giant financial services and management consultancies have started to recognise this, and it's one of the reasons we have seen such a huge growth in their acquiring design agencies to fast-track their design capability.

Brian Whipple, who was Global Managing Director of Accenture Interactive® at the time of the acquisition, said: 'In today's environment of digital disruption and heightened consumer expectations, the battle is for consumer engagement, and Accenture and Fjord® together will offer a deep blend of skills and expertise to help clients deliver innovative experiences that bridge marketing, commerce and service'.

Derrick Kiker, a McKinsey® partner who led the LUNAR acquisition, has similar sentiments about the power that design brings to an organisation: 'Until now, we couldn't help clients with design execution. Bringing together top design, engineering and business thinking in one holistic approach is going to be powerful'.

When Adaptive Path® was bought by financial services giant Capital One®, its Design Director, Jamin Hegeman, transitioned to become the Head of Design, Financial Services, at Capital One. He saw the acquisition as being triggered by a desire to quickly build up the corporation's nascent design capability:

> Increasingly, businesses are seeing the benefits of having design as a strong internal capability, and they're trying to bring it in-house. Acquisitions are a fast track to doing that; they're jump-starting a lack in that capability—whether it's a management consultancy who sees the benefit of having a design capability in their offering, or a large organisation that's been around awhile that wasn't built with a design capability at the start . . . Integrating design into an organisation is no small feat. Adding service design, which most organisations are still grappling to understand, is an even greater challenge.

Acquisitions certainly enable companies to fast-track capability gaps, but what about those designers caught up in the process? They're no longer working for the company they initially joined. Shelley Evenson was part of the design and innovation consultancy Fjord acquisition and is now Managing Director, Accenture Song. She saw many positives in terms of what she could achieve, and her work has taken on a scale that was not possible before:

> [The acquisition] gave Fjord a pretty incredible set of capabilities for thinking about implementation. Instead of just conceiving what things could be, it was about bringing them all the way through . . . What's interesting for me is that for most of my career, I've been really focused on thinking about how you integrate business, design and technology from the beginning. I feel like joining Accenture made that a huge possibility.

Unlike many other consultancies that have hit the headlines hard through acquiring design talent, Thoughtworks chose to take the longer and less public-facing approach. Why? Although it's often spoken about internally or during client pursuits, this is something that hasn't been documented . . . until now. Luckily, the Thoughtworks family tends to retain people over time, so I was able to extract the journey of design from Rebecca Parsons (Chief Technology Officer, Global), Ange Ferguson (Chief Transformation Officer, Global), Chad Wathington (Chief Strategy Officer, Global) and Kate Linton (Head of Design, Australia), all of whom have worked at Thoughtworks for between 10 and 20 years.

Back in 2003, Thoughtworks was a different company to what it is today. It was much smaller, with fewer than 1,000 people, and was therefore able to adapt quickly to change and the moving market. At the same time, it's always been a forward-looking company. They hired their first human–computer interaction (HCI) designer in the UK in 2003, and by 2006 they had designers in multiple countries. Rebecca says, 'We had to more broadly address the end-to-end process, and a design capability was crucial for that'. At the start, there were a number of local movements, with different regions seeing the need for design; then these movements began to accelerate and resonate more globally.

In 2009, they established the Thoughtworks University (TWU), a five-week intensive course undertaken by every new graduate, including designers. I asked Ange why they decided to grow their design capability:

> The way we've grown our capabilities has always been in service of how we can create better outcomes for our clients. Bringing in project management capabilities in the mid-2000s was in response to making sure we could continue to create value in the more complex client situations, and the motivation for design was similar. We saw a path to create greater value for clients, and we took it.

In talking about the reason for choosing organic growth rather than acquisition, Ange reflected the same sentiment and echoed some of the observations made by Kate:

> Organic capability growth has been central to our philosophy of talent development and expansion, driven in large part by a desire to ensure we maintain the culture of integration and collaboration in how we work, and we didn't see many design firms that took that approach.

Although growing organically is the longer path, it was the right decision for Thoughtworks, as Kate explains:

> We had experienced the pain of working with other designers who did not follow agile design practices but preferred to do a big up-front design and specification ahead of writing any code, uninformed by any technical feasibility or user research. Our designers have learnt to work in agile teams and have rapidly adopted continuous design practices, which enables teams to be more responsive to new information and de-risk projects by not over-investing in design prior to understanding the business, customer and technical context.

This has been the slower path and one that doesn't get the huge headlines—one that can both attract and deter design talent.

Whether taking an organic approach or the acquisition route, when a company moves in a new direction, there is always going to be a process to get people on board, and Thoughtworks was no exception. There was initial resistance, as integrating designers into delivery teams with developers exposed them to agile processes, and there were some false starts with design leaders in different countries. The integration relied on both designers and developers recognising each other as 'Thoughtworkers' and breaking down the barriers of the 'us vs them' mentality. Ange reflects:

> I think the designers had a tougher time than the pre-existing delivery role folks. At the time, integrating design with delivery was incredibly rare and was a big culture shock for those who were used to an agency approach. As with all new things, change is hard—it always will be. People gain confidence from successful experience, and it can be hard to ask people to step into an area that they have less confidence or experience in, whether it's how to sell, how to manage or how to execute.

While many have misunderstood what design thinking is or treated it as a tick box exercise, Thoughtworks used design thinking workshops to give people a basic understanding of the process. These added value by helping different capabilities recognise what design and delivery had in common and see that at the core it was creative problem solving—something they could all resonate with.

Overcoming resistance to new capabilities wasn't something new for Thoughtworks, which originated from pure agile technology roots. When business analysts, project managers and quality analysts were introduced over the years, they had the same resistance but overcame it. Then, in the early 2000s, when this design change was happening inside the organisation, developers only needed to know two or three coding languages, and mobile development was in its early stages; therefore, many of the developers felt team members needed to be generalists.

When Ange first joined the company in 2006, she was working with teams and recalls that most teams welcomed the shift to having design embedded, as they had been frustrated when design had been done by someone else in a way that was disconnected to delivery—and often unrealistic.

As already mentioned, the other advantage Thoughtworks had at the time was their size, so they could take the 'lean experiment' approach, which the company does on a regular basis with clients. Rebecca said that the way they got design to work with agile delivery was through trial and error, working together to figure out how to make design iterative: what needs to be decided early and how things flow through the process.

Ange added: 'Our size at the time was an advantage—it made sharing foundational experiences relatively simple and accelerated the ability to build on each set of experiences. It could be a different story at our current size (over 10,000)'. Design is much more holistic a capability than many of us realised. Ange also reflects:

> One insight was understanding the depth and breadth of roles within design. A common view when we began was that 'an XD is an XD is an XD', but through working with a

Design is much more holistic a capability than many of us realised.

whole range of designers, we all began to understand there were visual designers, experience designers, service designers and researchers . . . the list goes on.

During my research, it was interesting to hear that many designers across organisations or within consultancies still face this same problem today: a lack of knowledge and understanding about the complexity of design and the fact that not all designers are the same and there are specialisms. Designers still regularly have to explain the difference to clients, sales, business development managers and even those within their delivery teams.

Some voices have been louder than others in putting a flag in the ground and saying, 'Design is here', using either acquisition or organic growth as a PR opportunity to announce, 'Hey, we're changing, and this is how we do design and solve problems better than anyone else'. Regardless of who is flying the flag, all the articles really advocate for design and help push the message to other organisations, and for that I will always be appreciative. Even if it's a competitor getting the press, I salute them because every article is helping to break down the myths about design.

However, there is always another side to the story, and while some have struggled with acquisitions, others have simply failed to adopt the practices they advocate for. An insider once told me that they had been working for one of the large consultancies that openly advocated for and really pushed their world-class design practice. When they eventually met some of the designers from this highly publicised team, it turned out to be a much smaller group than had been suggested, and rather than getting access to users to test their ideas, the designers had to simply test on each other.

Nevertheless, the smoke and mirrors seemed to work—short term. Luckily for the design leaders within the consultancy, things changed when the CEO started to take an interest, and the consultancy is now far better off. I guess that demonstrates that sometimes in business you just have to be bullish enough to sell an idea and people will come. Once the idea proves to be something customers want, the positive PR will attract the best talent, and eventually those inside the organisation will see that it's worth investing in and start to back it. But if an organisation doesn't have the right leadership and backing for design, it's going to be a hard slog for any design leader.

Whether a business takes the pure organic approach, the acquisition approach or a blend of the two, all routes come with their challenges and rewards, which designers need to navigate in order to lead and change how design operates within an organisation. Ultimately, the successful integration of the design function eventually leads to designers' being able to scale, and—most important—the end experience for the user is enhanced, human-centred and delivers great products. The understanding of design will spread out across the many organisations that make up the client bases of these large consultancies—an audience that once would have been out of reach of the design world.

However, no organisation is perfect, and it can still be a frustrating process. What might be portrayed by self-promotion and through the media as glorious and smooth isn't always an accurate reflection of what's really going on under the hood!

The joining of these worlds has meant that not only have we all had to figure out new ways to work together, but consultancies have had to go on a journey to figure out how to sell their new approach to clients and show them best practice on how to integrate design successfully themselves. While organisations look to consultancies to help them with their journey, many don't even know they need a collaborative process—they still think they just have a technology problem or that a simple 'beautifying of the UI' will solve everything.

This is one of the many common challenges designers find in technology consultancies and companies, and they have to go from a designer to a DesignedUp leader in order to fundamentally change how organisations operate and see design. They need to first convince their client that it's a combined design and technology problem and then show a future vision of what their business and products could be like if they recognised it as such and were prepared to take action.

This is the journey you need to be ready to take your clients on.

It's not like these two worlds are so different. Both designers and developers are used to experimenting, testing to see what works, then iterating. The challenges are around getting the worlds to acknowledge that they're stronger together and working out the best way of designing and building at the same time.

For consultancies, the challenges are threefold: how to get design to work with their technology model, how to shift clients to a new way of thinking and how to get organisations to incorporate design at the centre of their business. There is then the shift the consultancy needs to take itself to ensure it is now building with a human-centred mindset—not everyone is a designer, but we all have the ability and responsibility to be user centred. So how do they sell the full end-to-end to clients? What story are they telling, and how can they ensure they can deliver great results across the entire journey to ensure continuity and best outcomes for clients and customers?

Design is not style. It's not about giving shape to the shell and not giving a damn about the guts. Good design is a renaissance attitude that combines technology, cognitive science, human need and beauty to produce something that the world didn't know it was missing.

Paola Antonelli, Senior Curator of the Museum of Modern Art

Designing in the new landscape

In the past, designers simply worked in design agencies. They didn't need to constantly justify the reason for design in-house because the agencies lived and breathed design, and that's what clients bought. They still needed to justify their costs and the value they were bringing, then pitch their ideas to clients; but that's the same in every business. However, many designers now, whether through choice or as a result of acquisition, find themselves in this new world in which they constantly have to justify themselves and what they do, both internally and externally.

Today's designers have to find ways to bring technology delivery teams along on the journey to understand design. They have to figure out how best to collaborate with agile teams and show badly functioning teams how to function better. They need to find ways to break down the barriers inside organisations to make them more customer centric and understand the value of design.

Some people—especially in government, procurement teams or other delivery teams—view design as a luxury and don't understand its value through the entire delivery process; yet ironically, many of these people will be regular users of Airbnb®, Uber® and other design-critical apps. For a designer working in a consultancy, this challenge raises its head with every new RFP, project and client. On top of this, they also need to navigate the world of consulting, especially if they've been acquired by a consultancy.

And then there's the work itself. Designers working in this world have to be fundamentally good at design and solving problems because that's what they're being paid to do. (Are you getting a picture of several plates spinning?) With so much going on, how can a designer lead effectively and not become bogged down with the complexities or overwhelmed with the sheer amount of stakeholder management and team uplift on top of the design work that's required of them? It is a real challenge—but one that can be overcome, I promise!

Bringing my vision to life

It's one thing to inspire and lead a client. However, influencing within the consultancy you work for is quite another.

I had just returned from five months' maternity leave after having my first child and was ready to get stuck in. I had a vision to create the first-ever design conference for Thoughtworks which would enable us to showcase our knowledge and expertise and demonstrate how we combine design and technology to create great experiences for customers and achieve amazing results for clients. I also wanted people to get a feel for how we work and position the Brisbane office at the front of potential clients' minds.

To get the initiative off the ground, I had to create a compelling reason and business plan, then present to finance and marketing to get their buy-in and secure funding. This involved managing many expectations, communicating with stakeholders and finding advocates across the organisation to support me. I needed to inspire people to join my cause and volunteer to help out, which meant I had to be clear with my vision from the outset. I then needed to manage the budget and really get people behind the vision.

Thoughtworks runs regular meet-ups across the different regions, which are free, with food and drinks provided—something many other design and technology organisations do. However, a meet-up is different to the type of event I envisioned, and because they're free, there is a huge drop-off rate. I didn't want my event to be just another freebie that could devalue our brand—I wanted people to value what we had to offer—so I created the first paid event in the history of Thoughtworks Australia. A year later, and after a lot of stakeholder management and planning, the first CXD (Customer Experience Design) conference was born in Thoughtworks. I referred to it as my second baby.

The event comprised:

- An executive lunch for attendees from the largest enterprises in Brisbane, with a keynote speaker from Thoughtworks
- A one-day conference with keynote speaker Rowan Lamont, Designworks Brisbane, who designed and manufactured the GC2018 Queen's Baton for the Commonwealth Games
- Interactive workshops, talks and a global panel discussion, bringing our design leaders from across the globe via Zoom® into the conference room to discuss and debate design and share their views and opinions on how to create differentiated customer experiences

Highlights:

- The first time pairing with one of the local businesses, Designworks
- The first time hosting a Thoughtworks design-focused conference
- Several follow-up meetings with prospective clients after the event, which enabled us to get some prospective clients over the line

Feedback from the event:

'I appreciated the hands-on workshop and international panel providing different perspectives'.

'I liked the mix of theory and how it has been applied practically in companies'.

'It was great to meet people in the industry in Brisbane and realise that we're all struggling with similar problems'.

As a design leadership step . . .

Throughout the process, everyone was supportive. The General Manager for Brisbane at the time, along with our Head of Design, critiqued my initial presentation and gave advice on where it could be improved before presenting it to our Head of Operations and Head of Marketing.

Thoughtworks had never conducted an event like this before, and I wasn't sure if marketing would be on board, but not only did they agree to support the event, they also gave me a great budget to work with and a dedicated person from their team to help. Fiona Byarugaba worked with me throughout to organise and plan the event—she was my rock and partner in crime throughout the whole process. I couldn't have done it without her and everyone else who helped make it a success.

My peers were excited and everyone got involved—developers, quality analysts, business analysts and, of course, the designers; we all came together to ensure the event was a success. The vibe in the office was unbelievable. We had a planning wall and daily standups; the website user journey was mapped on the wall and we had a small team on the beach working on its execution, with me as the product owner. From fixing technical problems and welcoming people to the event, to helping clean up, the incredible team effort ensured everyone had a fantastic time and we provided a great customer experience.

In terms of my career, I think it helped more people see my energy and what I could achieve, and I think it really helped other disciplines understand design. Karen Dumville, Global Head of Marketing Operations, Thoughtworks, shared this:

> In 2017, Emma came to me as Head of Marketing for Thoughtworks Australia (at that time), with an idea for a Customer Experience–focused event that would engage and educate the CX community in Brisbane. She had a clear vision for the format, content and execution and was passionate enough to persist in advocating for the event until she had company leadership support to go ahead. The vision became a reality and culminated in a full-day multi-stream event with 78 attendees across the conference and executive lunch. I congratulate Emma for her vision, passion and persistence in making the event a reality.

And Kate Linton, Head of Design, Thoughtworks, had these thoughts:

> Vision alone is never enough to really drive change. Project management skills, team leadership, delegation, negotiation and an eye for detail were all skills that Emma brought to this event to ensure success. Following CXD, Emma has gone on to advance her career and personal brand, both internally and externally, and is now a Principal at Thoughtworks and one of our key design luminaries.

Leaders formulate a vision of what great design can be for the organisation they are working with. I try to take my clients on a journey to show them what their product could be and get them excited about the vision. That initial momentum enables me to build a following and spread the love of design. Leaders also need to have followers throughout the organisation—it's crucial for design to succeed and for a customer-centric approach to technology to be truly embedded. As a consultant, you need to build a new tribe and find advocates for design with every new client. (I'll talk more about how to build your followers in Chapter 6.)

Design leadership and design management —What does it even mean?

If we look at managers in the traditional sense, their main focus is on building a team, managing that team and making sure they're effective at their jobs. They tend to have deeper structures with more formality and check-ins, and they protect their team from distractions that might come from other parts of the organisation, giving them the space to do their best work. Significantly, they are usually promoted into the position via a corporate 'career path', rather than emerging as naturally good leaders. This results in managers who might be loved or despised, with many simply viewed as 'okay'.

Leaders have to earn, rather than demand, respect and support from their peers. This relies on their being able to lean on the strong relationships and tribe they have built, using reasoned persuasion and a strong vision to make things happen. Effective leaders rely on their followers to help them achieve their vision—it's a team effort.

The role of the leader can be challenging and sometimes exhausting, always having to use persuasion and constantly justifying the reason for doing something. But having a team of people who are 'willing' rather than 'having' to help results in better outcomes, because when people feel they're part of a truly collaborative journey, they tend to put in much more effort and bring more ideas to the table. A design leader in a consultancy has to do this not only within the business, but also with every client. While that can take a lot of energy and effort, it's all a part of being a good design consultant, and the rewards can be tremendous.

While in conversation with Mike Mason (Global Head of Technology, Thoughtworks) about leadership, I was curious to find out what he thought made a good tech leader and if there were similarities with design leaders. 'One thing they do well is being able to bridge the roles', he said. 'Tech is specific with a lot of depth, like design, so you have to be able to communicate well with people who are not in your area'. I asked him specifically what he thought about one of our well-respected designers, Kate Linton, as a leader.

'A key factor in her success is that she is accomplished as a designer in her own right. This credibility helps her in her leadership role—having done the job you are meant to lead'.

> In some ways, leadership is more fluid and not a job description. You can have a group of people working on stuff, and someone naturally falls into the role of leader . . . Management and leadership is not everyone's strength.
>
> Mike Mason, Global Head of Technology, Thoughtworks

To make the transition from designer to a DesignedUp leader in a consultancy, you need to be able to do the design work while leading and managing the clients' expectations. Depending on the consultancy, you may also have to manage a cross-functional team. Clients will expect you to lead them in the new direction, which will require building a transparent and trusting relationship with your stakeholders, the tribe you have built and across the client's organisation. They will expect you to be able to design and most certainly will expect you to 'own the Sharpie' by stepping up and leading teams and discussions. This expectation that you will lead the client is simply part of being a consultant.

You won't be managing teams of designers or signing off designs; instead, you will be working collaboratively with your diverse team—which may or may not include other designers—leading them in the right direction and up-skilling team members on the value of being customer centric. Depending on the consultancy structure, you might not be directly responsible for other designers' performance reviews as a manager would be; however, you may be a coach for some designers, helping plan their goals for the year, giving advice and working with them on certain projects. Even with those around you who you're not specifically coaching, you will need to give guidance and advice on best practices. You're the guide, showing the team the way with design.

Once you are in a design leadership position within a consultancy, you will be involved in selling design to new clients, which, in turn, will help grow the design team. Leadership requires you to own and drive your own direction and set standards, and the consulting world lends itself to allowing people the room and flexibility (within reason) to do that.

After interviewing leaders across six of the largest global consulting firms, including the Big 4, I found that while they all share the same sentiment and opportunities, their paths to get there often differ, with some providing more support for design growth than others.

Now, if you're ready to step up within your organisation, or if you're already leading in some capacity but want to build your skills and learn more about how you can work and lead more effectively in this new world, read on!

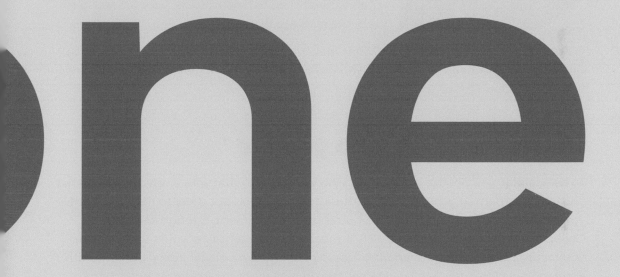

designedUp traits

Not everyone can be or wants to be a design leader, but those who can or do show similar traits. Leaders tend to emerge naturally because of these traits, and by fostering them, they are able to influence organisations and grow tribes. Some traits are shared by all leaders, regardless of sector, and sometimes we have to get perspectives from non–design leaders in order to understand leadership more fully and see common traits we may not have thought about or appreciated before.

esign leaders pave the way, they are not afraid to carve a new path or try something new. Design Leaders are not managers who have been appointed by those higher up, they are chosen by those around them, they build followers, instil inspiration and in the consulting world they lead clients through the journey of understanding designs value and bringing the humans, the users and the customers into the business and technology world to solve the real problem. They do this for both the clients and the consultancy, taking every opportunity to bring others into their world. And while they emerge naturally, organisations need to help nurture, support and give them the space to blossom.

Before I delve into the specifics of what makes a design leader, let's strip things back, because you first need to establish who you are, where your natural strengths lie and how you respond to the things work and life throw your way.

Understanding who you are

To be a leader, you need to understand who you are and what your strengths are so that you can put them to good use. While there are many tools out there to help you identify your personality type, I find the CliftonStrengths® assessment, StrengthsFinder®, by Gallup the most useful (see Figure 1.1). It measures the intensity of your talents to help you focus on your strengths, and the assessment is under constant development, with extra tools and features being added all the time. Many of the leaders I spoke to from some of the largest consultancies have taken the assessment more than once over the years to see whether things have changed.

Mike Mason, Global Head of Technology, Thoughtworks, is a fan of the tool. He related:

> CliftonStrengths helped explain some things about me and my personality. Understanding yourself better is really important because it helps you understand what motivates you and the kinds of things you're going to remain committed to. And not every 'strength' is actually 100% positive.

> For example, one of my strengths is I'm an achiever, which sounds great, but it can be super-negative if I don't feel like I've achieved something for the day. Understanding that helped with my self-management, and I learned to think about things in a way that gives me little rewards as I go along.

Back when I was a programmer, I could get a story card off the wall and implement it—red/green/refactor/desk check; every time somebody said 'Yep' or 'Okay', it was like little achievement cookies all day long. Moving from that to a leadership role, you tend to go from feeling like you're accomplishing stuff to being in meetings all day and feeling like you're not actually accomplishing anything, so you've just got to find new achievement and reward markers. At the moment, I have loads of stickies on the bottom of my monitor that I'm pulling off before the Christmas break, and I'm refusing to add any more.

Being someone who likes to reward myself with chocolate, I asked Mike how he was going to reward himself after he'd gotten rid of all the notes. He replied: 'Well, just the fact that the stickies are gone, that's my reward'. Very disciplined of him!

Figure 1.1 StrengthsFinder domains as adapted from Strengths Based Leadership, Rath and Conchie, 2008, Gallup, Inc. (Adapted with kind permission of Gallup, Inc.)

My own strengths

When I conducted StrengthsFinder, my five areas of strength were:

Achiever
Futuristic
Competition
Significance
Positivity

I can completely resonate with what Mike says. After doing my StrengthsFinder and speaking to one of my close friends, it turned out we both share the same 'Achiever' trait and need that achievement cookie every day, which explains why we both get such satisfaction from ticking things off our 'to do' lists. I also merge my 'Achiever' and 'Competition' traits—and when I say competition, I don't mean against my peers, I mean against myself.

How can I make this better than last time, how can I push this further, how can I get approval to do this or that? While I can't always get that competitive satisfaction through my work, I love exercise, so doing a spin or gym class or going for a run gives me that extra buzz, because it ticks both the achievement and competitive goals. It can be as simple as 'I've achieved a run today', or it might be that I beat my last time or went a bit further—it's just about setting a goal and achieving it. Harnessing your strengths doesn't have to be restricted to work, so why not get your achievement cookies over the weekend?

The 'Positivity' attribute is definitely something I hadn't noticed before, but looking back on my career and where I am today, it's clear. And the feedback I've had from peers reflects it, such as this from a co-worker: 'Despite multiple signs that this [pitch] was going to end up a fruitless waste of our valuable time, you never demurred or showed any sign of losing your dignity, energy and style. The persistence paid off, we changed the client's mind and ultimately won what is now a successful account. I learnt a lot about keeping going from that'.

I think this is a strength that can really help in the design and tech world; no matter what you're faced with, being positive helps you face some of your clients' biggest challenges and encourages those around you to feel that everything is going to be ok. At the same time, I recognise the need to ensure I balance this, especially when there is a huge risk involved and I could come across as being blasé.

The 'Futuristic' trait can be both a positive and a negative. As design leaders, we need to paint the vision of the future and create the 'North Star' that our team can align with and get excited about. Having that vision is what keeps me going—it's what helps me get through the challenges we face on projects and within organisations. However, we also need to accept that some people will view this attitude as overreaching and perceive it to be that designers are always pushing to enhance the user's experience with little regard for cost.

So, while our job is to always push for the best, backed up with data and research, we design leaders just need to make a conscious effort, especially when working remotely, to ensure that the people who matter see the whole picture—that they also hear those conversations where we suggest simplifying something to stay within budget and time, or when we're working with developers to find a solution to a problem that was simply not foreseen. It's a case of showing that yes, as design leaders we're always striving to drive the user experience forward and solving the right problem, but we're also very much on board with bringing in projects on spec and within viable parameters.

With any assessment, what's most important is your reaction to it. Ask yourself: 'Why am I responding this way?' You might not agree with everything, but you will find things that resonate and explain some of the feedback you may have gotten. It allows you to reflect on who you are and why you act the way you do.

We often forget to reflect on what we have achieved, where we are and where we want to go. I'm definitely bad at doing this because I'm always pushing forward and striving for the next thing, but that's my Competition and Achiever traits coming through! Considering the results of the assessment really allowed me to understand myself better so I could work on creating a career path that would stop the constant itch and satisfy my personality.

The assessment also enabled me to understand why I sometimes feel restless at the end of the day if I haven't achieved something—which drives my husband crazy! To solve this, I set myself targets within my regular fitness regime, which allows me to somewhat balance my competitive side, especially at points when I feel my career is standing still.

Like many other people with similar leadership traits, I'm just impatient! And the technology advancements that have enabled me to track my fitness better have also tapped into my competitive side, to the point where if Google® Maps says it will take me 50 minutes to walk somewhere, I'll try to do it in 40.

The best advice I've had on how to apply myself came from one of my coaches, who said: 'Work on your strengths and nurture what you have; don't waste time and energy focusing on what you don't have'. But while it is advisable to double down on your strengths, it's also important not to ignore all your weaknesses. Maria Gomez, Director of Engineering at BCG Digital Ventures in Berlin, has completed the assessment twice and says:

> I found things that were not my strength the first time around now are a strength. It's good to put your strengths on the table, as there might be some gaps you need to work on to help you get where you want to go. I can lack gravitas in meetings. To solve this, I now prepare ahead of time and think about the kind of questions I might get. This helps me prepare my answers and thoughts in advance, rather than stumbling and trying to find my words in the meeting.

Tech Principal Kevin Yeung (Tech Principal at Thoughtworks when I interviewed him, now Head of Data Platform at 3P Learning), who did the StrengthsFinder at the same time as I did, then took the assessment again a while later to validate it, has a different perspective:

> It's like the horoscope—the descriptions are so broad you can always find something that resonates. I did find it interesting, although I'm not sure it was accurate. But focusing on your strengths does make sense; it has helped me make decisions on what to do and not do and helped me say no to the things I'm not good at.

So, even 'non-believers' benefit!

Don't ask for permission

When a design leader sees a problem—whether it's inside their organisation or when working with a client—rather than leaving it to someone else to sort out, they seek ways to influence change, close the gap and solve the problem. They tend to take the 'Grace Hopper' approach*: *It's easier to ask forgiveness than it is to get permission!*

This is particularly important when working as a consultant because your purpose is to influence and drive change within the team and client you're working with. And the beauty of being onsite with the client and immersing yourself in their organisation is that you're able to influence much more widely than if you were at an agency working in silo and only presenting to the client every few weeks.

One of our clients had a variety of products all aimed at solving problems for the same industry and a 20-plus-year-old legacy system. The project involved reimagining one of the key products, which would then set the direction for how all the other products would eventually look and function.

While conducting customer research, it became apparent that customers referred to the company by the product we were reimagining, rather than the actual company name, and they also didn't know the individual names of the other various products within the suite. There was a disconnect between the client's marketing team and the digital product teams and a lack of consistent brand direction across their suite of products and marketing materials.

It quickly became clear to me that unless we had a clear vision of how the products were going to work together in the future and created consistent branding across all the products in the ecosystem, there would be a big problem. We would soon need to either hold back delivery due to lack of clear direction, launch a product that did not reflect who the brand was, or create something that would eventually require a lot of rework once a consistent branding had been prioritised—which could possibly even mean renaming the product.

---

* American computer scientist and US Navy rear admiral, created the programming language that was later extended to become COBOL. https://en.wikipedia.org/wiki/Grace_Hopper

Although branding solutions wasn't something Thoughtworks offered at that time, recognising the risks based on my experience enabled us to raise the concerns with the team and client. The client saw themselves as a technology company, and the focus had been on building products. They hadn't considered how their products sat together, how customers differentiated among them, and they didn't fully understand how branding worked.

Bringing my branding experience together with customer insights and the risks to the project, I ran a series of short branding workshops with key stakeholders to align the different teams and get an agreement on our vision and direction.

From the information we gathered in these workshops and from customer research, I was able to encapsulate who they really were as a brand, defined a brand vision, strategy, brand values, a brand architecture for their suite of products, a brand style guide which included new product brand colours that met accessibility guidelines and a roadmap. This work would bring much-needed consistency to their products, reduce confusion for customers and enable us to move forward as a team and remove some of the project risks and blockers.

For the first time, the designers in the product teams and marketing started talking, and the CTO and CMO began thinking differently about the future of their products. I created a small team of people who could own the new direction and continue with what I had started once my part in the project was over.

This is the kind of problem solving and added value that design leaders bring to their clients. We grab the reins and combine our skills, experience and leadership traits to imagine a new direction and show them the way forward. Design and tech leaders are stewards. So, if you see a problem you're sure you can fix, don't be afraid to go ahead without seeking permission. It's also often easier to show the advantages of the solution once you've found it than trying to explain your vision from behind the challenge.

The power of praise and recognition

A leader who inspires others understands that while money is a motivator, so are praise, recognition, rewards and a simple 'Thank you'. Acknowledging an individual's contribution and the value of their work plays a huge part in building and nurturing their self-esteem. They need to believe that at the end of the journey you're taking them on, they are going to be recognised and rewarded for their efforts. Having team members feel valued leads to a much better working environment and builds a loyal tribe of followers who will willingly help you achieve your vision and goals.

So, as a leader, you must be open and honest about the risks and rewards of following a particular path so that your team can understand what's in it for them. As designers, we are well versed in empathy and understanding pain points, but we need to use these tools—which we already apply every day with our customers—on our own team members and people across the organisations we work with. Once you really understand what people expect, you'll be able to better identify and articulate the things that should motivate and drive them.

Give credit where credit is due

There is nothing better for your team's morale than giving public credit to individuals within it, so openly praise the person who had the idea or carried out the work, and don't ever take credit for something you didn't do. That said, some people are uncomfortable with public praise. In that case, if they have a coach or mentor, you can give the positive feedback to them in the presence of the person—tell the coach how impressed you are, etc. A technical leader at one of the Top 4 consultancies agrees: 'Telling someone they've done well makes them feel great, but doing it in a public way, even if it's by email and cc-ing others in, is really powerful'.

Thoughtworks have monthly update meetings where company news and events are shared. Part of this meeting includes recognition awards for each region, focusing on consultants that are doing great work. In Brisbane, where I'm based, it's the Pineapple award (they all have fun names), and I've always made a conscious effort to nominate different people. The awards require the winner to have the highest number of nominations, so I encourage other team members to nominate the individual if I know they feel the same as I do.

Exercise: What do you appreciate about the person next to you?

To . . .
Name of person you are giving appreciaton to.

I really appreciate . . .
Write one or two things you appreciate about the person, such as:

Thank you for always bringing new ideas and sharing best practices with the team. Most of all, your attention to detail in general has been nothing short of awesome. Keep up the great work.

From . . .
Name of person giving the appreciaton.

Figure 1.2   Team building exercise using praise

Encouraging others to share praise helps create a strong team, builds morale and fosters appreciation amongst team members. One of the exercises I particularly like is that during a team group session, everyone spends a few minutes writing down what they appreciate about the person next to them, then you go round in a circle, and everyone shares what they have written (see Figure 1.2). If you have a large team or have been conducting back-to-back workshops, you can split people up and do the same exercise in small groups.

Food is another great way to reward people for their efforts or to encourage a team when things are tough. I was working with a pair of developers who were trying to fix lots of UI issues, and I knew they liked a particular chocolate milkshake, so I made sure they had a good supply while they worked.

On another project, we had a lot of tech hurdles to fix. While I couldn't help with the issues, I knew I could bring encouragement, so I bought a large cake from a specialist French patisserie and got the team to down tools for a few minutes. They enjoyed some cake, while I assured them we were going to get through it. Mike Mason advises:

> If you show appreciation with food, make it memorable. When I got my pilot's licence, I brought gourmet doughnuts to the flight office for everyone to enjoy.

Figure 1.3 Jelly Modern Doughnuts.
@jellymodern | jellymoderndoughnuts.com
(Licensed under Flickr Creative Commons at
https://www.flickr.com/people/127082525@N06/

Followers and trust

Design leaders have an endless passion for and belief in what they do—they're always trying to make the world a better place through the use of design. That passion, together with vision and the ability to build trust with the people around them, enables them to attract followers—a tribe that wants to learn and build their vision. As I said earlier, many managers are put into a place of authority by a system, and they make people do what they want through enforcing the hierarchy. Leaders are different because they've earnt their followers.

It requires trust to drive design change in an organisation, to recruit willing followers to help in your quest and make the introverts feel safe. This doesn't happen overnight, but it must happen quickly, especially in a fast-paced agile delivery team. And the good news is, building trust really isn't complicated. In my experience, you simply need to be honest, open, empathetic and, most important, nice.

Removing the obstacles

Not only do design leaders have endless passion, they also fight tirelessly for both their team and the end users, who want a superb experience. As consultants, it's our job to remove the obstacles inside our clients' organisations, show them the way forward and build strong advocates for design within their ranks.

As design leaders in a tech consultancy, we also have the added task of finding advocates inside our own organisation. We need to build followers and trust both internally and externally, which is double the effort and often frustrating and tiring, but that's where our endless passion comes into play.

We need to serve as the loudspeaker for the other design consultants, many of whom may be finding their way inside a technology or business consultancy for the first time. We need to be their voice, understand their frustrations, lead them in the right direction and try to break down obstacles on their behalf.

One of the problems Thoughtworks faced globally was trying to sell more of the right type of design work and put more designers into delivery teams. A small group of us came together across three cities and compared the issues we were facing. We then put together a list of some specific issues we wanted to fix and discussed who would be the best advocate for us.

At the time, a new head of sales had been appointed, so we jumped at the opportunity to get him on board. Luckily, he was open to the idea and also had a genuine desire to improve how design was sold, so he agreed to let us run a short training session to up-skill the sales team on design. The city I worked in had a smaller office, so I was able to work closely with our salespeople, and we didn't have nearly as many issues as the other larger offices.

Being part of the Global Design Team gave me an understanding of what other countries were doing and the challenges they faced. I knew the UK was going through similar problems, so rather than duplicating work, I reached out to them to see what they had learnt and if they had solved the problem. They were happy to pass over the presentation and workshop they had run with their sales team, which allowed us to quickly get ahead by simply adapting their content for our own market and problems.

I worked with our designers and sales team to create a more focused version for our city, specifically highlighting areas we wanted to tackle. Doing this helped give our designers a voice, which was a big deal for those who spent a lot of time out of the office on client projects and who were therefore not always in a position to help change things inside the consultancy.

I paired with another design leader from the Sydney office, and together we ran a presentation and workshop session with the Australian sales team, who are across three offices in different cities. We walked them through the state of design in Australia, and to make it more relevant to each city, I highlighted key accounts where design had already been a success and where there were opportunities to grow design.

The workshop allowed us to hear the sales team's views and understand their pain points. They were engaged, shared some great stories about design and were also keen to learn from us. After the session, the head of sales asked if we could add the findings to a presentation he was preparing to give to the management team and MD of Australia. These were then used to create objectives for the business in the following financial year.

Jennifer Martin is Associate Partner | Asia Pacific Experience Design Leader, EY,

When demand exceeds supply, you've got your business case for more designers.

responsible for expanding the practice of design and design thinking within EY in Asia Pacific. She launched and leads EY wavespace, a service that brings the best of EY tools, people and technology into bespoke experiences to collaboratively solve client problems. Prior to that, she was the Director of IBM Studios in Melbourne. I spoke with her about her approach to removing obstacles and instilling design inside a consultancy.

One of her key approaches to 'selling design', whether within the consultancy or with a client, is to understand their social style—are they more analytical or emotional? This approach of tailoring communication based on the audience was common among all the leaders I spoke to; however, Jennifer takes it a step further for 'must win' conversations by recording herself to rehearse. This helps her refine the story she wants to tell, which reduces nerves and the chance of the 'Imposter Syndrome' creeping in—more on that shortly.

Another way Jennifer has instilled design inside a consultancy is by demonstrating the value added by a design-led approach. 'Identify your stakeholders' problems and show them how design (and designers) can help. When demand exceeds supply, you've got your business case for more designers'.

Give solutions, not problems

As designers, we are well versed in solving problems. We do it constantly—our minds are always focused on asking questions and figuring out how we would do something better. That might be asking ourselves how we can design a better experience for the customer in the app we're working on; working out the best way to help our client overcome resistance and scale design across their organisation; thinking about new ways to find advocates—or even questioning why some vending machines dispense the item you have purchased low down, meaning you have to bend over to fish out your item from behind the resistant flap! Problem solving is in our nature, yet time and again, I hear designers complaining about how design works inside their organisation and expecting someone else to solve the problem.

Design leaders never simply point out when something's not working; they address the problem and offer a solution—sometimes several! So, if you're not sure how to resolve an issue, grab the bull by the horns and steer it into a brainstorm. Discuss the problem and carry out some research to find both short- and long-term solutions.

It's important that you back up your ideas with facts and data wherever possible. This can be gained from a number of areas: findings from user testing; data that call centres collect on the types of calls and customer problems; data that legal departments have as they write the legislation and T&Cs; sales data on what's selling, customer reactions and what customers want; analytics you might have built into your products . . . and so on.

> ## Facts and data will win over marketing teams. It takes out the emotion.
> Linda Goldstein, Executive Vice President of Customer Experience and Marketing at CSAA. Forrester CX Podcast

There should be plenty of evidence to support your proposed solution, but finding it all will require you to have the right relationships or to seek out the people who can help you. If you explain *why* you need the information, you should find people will be more than happy to help you succeed.

Depending on the severity of the problem and who you're presenting your proposed solutions to, there are a number of ways you can go about it and plenty of frameworks online you can use. Below is one I have created to help map out the problem, the risk and both short- and long-term options. This helps the business take an incremental approach and gives them various choices (see Figure 1.4).

The problem(s)
(customer, employee, tech, business)

The risks
(to the business and customers)

	COST	PRO'S	CON'S	IMPACT
Short term options				
Long term options				

Figure 1.4   One framework for mapping out problem and solutions

Before you present the problem and possible solutions, take some time to think about it from the viewpoint of the person or people you're presenting to. What do they care about? If you were in their shoes, how would you want to be told this information? This is what Jennifer Martin is doing when she thinks about whether her audience is more analytical or emotional. The more empathetic you can be with those receiving the information, the more likely it is you'll be able to engage in a useful dialogue with them, especially if the issue that needs resolving is in an area that's not their specialism.

Mike Mason said that if he's receiving bad news, he would certainly want to know that the person had already thought about options on how to solve the problem. He also talked about the importance of timing: 'When you deliver bad news, never do it on a Monday, Friday or when the client is just about to get on a flight to go home for the weekend. That just sucks!'

Sometimes we can become so focused on resolving the problem, particularly if it's time sensitive, that we just want to fire ahead and get moving with an agreed solution. But, although being eager to present our proposals to the relevant person might be admirable, it's important to remember that there are other things going on in their lives. The bigger the potential bombshell, the greater the need to gauge the timing of the news to get the best response.

When discussing this topic with Kevin Yeung, while he advocates for focusing on the stakeholder's situation and having empathy for them, he points out the need to also consider the problem from an organisational viewpoint:

> Delivering 'bad news' should really be, 'We've exhausted all options at our pay grade and need your help'. If we need to tell a stakeholder they are doing the wrong thing, frame their action as an option alongside your recommendations. Point out the trade-offs and consequences of each option. Sometimes, people make bad choices because they didn't have the right information and are happy to switch if given a tractable way out.

It is certainly advisable to bear in mind that the person you are presenting to may not know they are doing the wrong thing; they may also have an agenda that you are not aware of. Once you have identified a problem, get started working on solutions right away, but take a pause before presenting to make sure that you deliver those solutions at the right time and in the right way for your audience.

No elitists here, please

This is a short but important point. No one wants to be 'the seagull', who comes in and, as author Jared Spool would say, 'swoops and poops' all over your work. That person you're slightly afraid to have a conversation with or an opinion around; the one that doesn't chip in and get their hands dirty when you're up against it. As a design leader, if you want to gain the respect of everyone around you, never ask them to do things you wouldn't do yourself.

This is especially important in the consulting world, where some might have already mentally put us on the elitist stool before we've even walked in the door. We need to be humble and show we are there to help as part of their team—we're not trying to work against them or make their life more difficult.

The importance of having humility was something that came up during several conversations with design and tech leaders about design leadership traits. You have to be confident that you are an expert in your area while understanding that you are just one piece of the puzzle—you've got to be able to accept constructive criticism and suggestions from non-designers. A technical leader at one of the Top 4 consultancies reflected:

> Technologists want the same things as designers: We want to create something that works, does the job and delights the user. Let's look at the things that we have in common and align us. If they incorporate other views, that is when magic happens.

Instil inspiration

One of the things I love about design leadership is instilling inspiration. As a DesignedUp leader, you need to share your passion in a way that enables others to feel passionate too. Watching a team form around a vision and mission is powerful, and the drive and determination of that team can have a huge impact across the whole organisation.

As a design consultant, this could be something as simple as instilling the passion for usability testing across your development team. You can then take it wider by bringing other departments into the conversation and inspiring them to be passionate about usability testing as well. Getting people to 'learn by doing' brings them along on the journey, helps spread your mission and has a far wider impact on the organisation.

Case study

We were helping a client navigate the largest digital transformation project the organisation had ever undertaken. I was the only designer on the 25-person team that needed to deliver the goods with design and take the organisation on the human-centred journey—something they had never done before. As part of the work, I needed to conduct user research across our identified cohorts for a minimum viable product (MVP). The research and findings needed to be completed within one iteration (two weeks), and I was only working four days a week (entertaining my toddler on the fifth day!).

Within just eight days, we managed to conduct 19 one-on-one customer interviews, make 305 observations and run a co-design workshop. This was achieved by explaining to my team, the customer engagement team and marketing how the research would contribute to achieving our overall vision and mission. We reassured them that I would train them personally, paired with other senior Thoughtworkers on our team who were comfortable conducting this type of research.

Encouraging them to tread the path unknown and getting them excited and focused on the end goal enabled me to recruit a team of enthusiastic helpers. This equipped us to gather the research we needed quickly and start the process of instilling design and customer centricity across the organisation, not just within our team.

I've always found that people are happy to help out as long as the process and end goal is properly explained and they're clearly walked through exactly what is expected of them and what they need to do.

To inspire people to help, you need to make sure they feel included and that their work has purpose and meaning. Generally speaking, delivery teams, customer support and marketing teams are keen to create products that customers love too, so if you can foster and encourage a shared passion for the mission, that will create a feeling that 'we're all in this together', and people will feel it's a safe place to push boundaries in order to achieve the mission.

> **The actions that you take every day at work are powerful beyond your wildest dreams. So make sure that your actions are inspirational and call out the best from your people.**
>
> Anonymous

Imposter Syndrome

This is a self-imposed psychosis, where—even if only temporarily —you feel as though you're not good enough, you're 'bluffing' your way through each day with no real idea what you're doing, and you could be 'found out' at any moment. I think it happens to most

people at some point, and it's easy to let it get the better of us, particularly because it can creep up so fast that we don't always notice it until the last minute.

I've found that women are usually more open about the Imposter Syndrome, and it's especially common in women returning to work after having children—certainly it was something I suffered when I went back after having my second child. That surprised me, as I hadn't experienced it the first time around, and I can only put that down to the fact that I was part of a leadership development programme the first time, which I continued while on maternity leave. I therefore came back to work with a clear mission, vision and goal on what I wanted to achieve—plus, as it was my first child, I was determined to prove that I could have a career and be a mum!

But with my second child, I was trying to figure out how I could successfully balance life and work with two children while also being uncertain about what was next for my career. I never told anyone how I felt, I just put on a brave face and tried my best to ignore this thing in the back of my head saying, 'You're not good enough'.

The saving grace for me was my passion around design leadership and having something to focus on as a kind of therapy to carry me through how I was feeling. And that thing was writing this book!

During my research, I asked leaders from design and tech if they ever suffered from Imposter Syndrome, and there was no hesitation from anyone—they all immediately said: 'Yes, all the time!' So, if you start to doubt yourself, remember that everyone experiences this at some point, even people at the top of their game. And the reality is, if you weren't good enough, you wouldn't have been hired in the first place, so never be afraid to lead and be heard.

> ### The Imposter Syndrome isn't as strong as it once was, but I actually don't want to lose it completely—I don't want to become cocky!
>
> Evan Bottcher, Head of Architecture, MYOB

While discussing the topic with Evan Bottcher, I really liked that he feels that the odd burst of Imposter Syndrome helps keep him human and grounded. I'd never heard anyone talk about it like that before, and I think it's a really helpful way of reframing the feeling.

Mike Mason has been in the industry for a long time and has a wealth of experience, but he still suffers from Imposter Syndrome. 'I suffer from it all the time. Our CEO Guo Xiao, Gary O'Brien and I had spent two years creating the Digital Fluency Model,* yet when

---

* O'Brien, G., Xiao, G. and Mason, M. (2019). *Digital Transformation Game Plan: 34 Tenets for Masterfully Merging Technology and Business.* O'Reilly Media. ISBN: 978-1492054399.

I was due to talk about it to the Global CTO of a client in New York, I was so nervous I couldn't sleep the night before. The meeting went well, and the client stayed longer than the intended hour. Afterwards, I was talking to Cassie (Cassandra Shum, Head & Technical Director of Cloud Partnerships at Thoughtworks NY at the time and now VP of Field Engineering, RelationalAI) and told her how incredibly nervous I'd been and that I couldn't sleep. She was surprised and said she couldn't tell. Personally, I think if you're not nervous about something like that, you've either done it a million times before or you don't care enough about it'.

I can completely relate to this. If I'm presenting for the first time or it's a new conference, I can never sleep and always worry I'll mess it up or not make sense. My worst fear—and I think it's a common one—is being asked questions I don't know the answer to. It seems a level of nerves when it comes to important events is almost unavoidable; the key to keeping them under control is preparing well and remembering that the reason you've been chosen to be in the room is that you know your stuff.

If you're one of the many designers from an agency that has been acquired by a tech or business company/consultancy, then your job is to show them why you were hired. Remember that they probably know little about design, so you have the advantage of being the most qualified person in the room. You can teach them about what you do and why it's important, but always make sure you can back up your arguments with evidence and clearly demonstrate how the design function and your own skills and expertise are going to benefit them.

> **If you're not nervous about doing something, you've either done it a million times or you don't care.**

As design leaders, on top of dealing with our own Imposter Syndrome and insecurities, we also have to help others deal with theirs. Jennifer Martin (Associate Partner | Asia Pacific Experience Design Leader, EY) has observed that junior designers and consultants often feel their contributions aren't relevant, so they don't speak up in meetings and workshops, instead waiting to share their ideas privately afterwards. So she opens workshops with, 'We want this to be a brave space where everyone is comfortable sharing and collaborating', and she engages people directly to give everyone an opportunity to participate.

You need to be okay to speak up; as the saying goes: 'The only stupid questions are the ones you don't ask'. We learn by asking, and if you have a query, you can almost guarantee at least one other person in the room will be wondering the same thing. In workshops, I find it can be helpful to run a quick feedback session at the end, where people write on post-its what worked, what didn't work and anything that puzzled them. Everyone sticks them on a board or wall so we can run through the comments and address any queries. This can help give a voice to those who aren't comfortable speaking up and perhaps encourage them that other people will always have questions too.

On this subject, Evan told me,

> I'm always apologising for not being organised and structured. Between 2006 and 2010, when I was a tech lead, especially when I was working with one of our large banking clients, every time a tech lead joined the team, I thought they were better than I was. I kept saying: 'I'm not the right person to be doing this, I can't do this every day'. Then I would go ahead and do it.

As a self-confessed perfectionist, I regularly have to remind myself to let go. Of course, you should always try to do a great job, but it's equally important to forgive yourself when the inevitable mistakes happen. We are all human, and nobody is perfect 100% of the time. This is especially true when creating digital products and services, because by no means is everything plain sailing in the creation of digital solutions. DesignedUp leaders have to learn to let go when the technology just can't do what you want it to do or when a customer workshop doesn't go quite as well as the last one.

Failure is only the opportunity to begin again more intelligently.

Henry Ford

So don't wait until you feel completely confident to start putting yourself out there. Courage comes from taking risks and many a successful leader used the 'fake it 'til you make it' principle on their way up. Many high achievers actually view it as a skill because they thrive on the challenge of the unknown.

Getting bankers to sketch!

I hadn't been working at Thoughtworks for long when I was asked to run my first 'client discovery'. This is a series of research and design activities that enable us to understand the problem(s) that need solving and uncovering the business, customer and technical contexts, opportunities and constraints. It involves researching the problem space, framing the problem, considering potential solutions and gathering evidence to shape the solution.

The discovery phase typically lasts a few weeks, which leads into inception, which again consists of workshops and helps the team get started with delivery. Discovery doesn't simply stop at the beginning of delivery—it continues throughout the process to ensure that what is delivered continues to solve the problems uncovered along the way.

In this case, not only was it my first Client Engagement Lead position for Thoughtworks, but it was for a group of 30 executive bankers at a large account we were trying to win. No pressure! I had a good team around me, so I wasn't worried about running the discovery—I'd acted as Client Engagement Lead when I ran my own business. The challenge was getting the approach right: I was told they didn't like co-design and sketching—it had been tried before and failed, so there was no point in attempting it. But I needed to get them out of their comfort zones and to think creatively about what was possible.

Having researched different solutions, I came across the Silly Cow business innovation exercise by Strategyzer®—a fun activity designed to unleash people's creative juices to generate innovative ideas, where teams create and sketch an innovative business based on the characteristics of a cow (see Figure 1.5). It is designed to encourage out-of-the-box thinking and helps prepare participants for an ideation session focused on the organisation's specific needs.

Figure 1.5   Silly Cow exercise (images created by the author)

The exercise has had great reviews and had been conducted with execs before, so I decided I would try it. It was a high risk, and no one in the company had used it before (to my knowledge), but I had planned the session well and went with my gut feeling that I could get a group of exec bankers to sketch!

Well, it couldn't have gone any better. In fact, it went so well that I've used the same approach with many clients since. The bankers loved the exercise—it enabled them to think differently and got them excited about what the future could be for their own problem. They came up with some truly creative Silly Cow business ideas, and we went on to develop several great MVP options to solve their business problem during the ideation sketching that followed.

They are now one of our key accounts, and, although that's not directly down to the Silly Cow exercise (if only winning clients were that easy!), I like to think that the work we did helped towards gaining their trust. It's an example of why sometimes you just have to go with your gut and 'do' rather than ask. Mike Harris, who created three iconic billion-pound brands, was a mentor of mine, and I live by his saying:

> If something doesn't excite and scare you,
> you need to change the game you're playing.

Understanding users drives great design

We all know that understanding users drives great design, and as design leaders, we need to use this to our advantage. Understanding what motivates clients will allow you to have more meaningful conversations and present the case for design in a more compelling way that will make things happen.

For instance, C-level executives don't like to be bothered with the details, they just want the high-level information and for it to solve a problem that is currently on their radar. Get to the point quickly, and show clearly what advantage your solution gives the business. This kind of understanding and empathy with the client can also be used to build trust and improve relationships that may have been difficult in the past.

For example, one client had a particular cohort who was notoriously difficult to work with. The relationship had been strained over the years, and they constantly played the blame game. The first research and design workshop we ran with them was part of their quarterly face-to-face get together, and they had advised it would be the best way to conduct some of the research.

They were the hardest group of people I'd had to work with so far. Many of them simply refused to engage. They hated sketching and couldn't see the value because they didn't care about design and saw it as our problem to solve. I explained that we needed to gather insights to help us design a solution that they would like and find intuitive. I stressed that our aim was to design something that would solve their problems and make the tasks they had to complete easier and faster—and to achieve that we needed their input.

Some of the more forward-thinking people in the group approached me later and said they liked the session and could see the value, but there were others with a narrower mindset. So, in the second session with these users, we changed things—for instance, as they specifically asked not to use post-its or sketch, we instead printed out screens from the original system and facilitated gathering information on how they used it. This session proved much better, but I still wasn't happy, and I felt we weren't getting the insights we needed. However, by this stage we'd built a good relationship with the client and understood some of the personalities and challenges of this particular cohort much better.

The users were from different organisations, and although it had originally appeared they were all aiming for the same thing, it emerged that they actually were rivals. The smaller organisations didn't want to voice their opinions in front of the larger ones, and the larger organisations felt like they had more power, as they had people from their side on the board of directors for our client. And while the board members were meant to be impartial, they had been using their powers to drive their own agendas, rather than making decisions for the good of everyone.

I suggested to the client that we conduct some contextual inquiries to allow us to build bridges, gain trust and give us richer insights into the users' needs. This new direction worked well with the cohort and enabled us to find out things we never would have by using the original approach. The users were much better one on one than in a group and shared a lot more information with us. The client also saw the advantage and the relationships improved.

So, if your first approach doesn't work, don't be afraid to change direction and try something different. As design leaders, we must recognise when something isn't working and keep adjusting until something sticks that gives us the outcome we're aiming for. Using our design knowledge together with customer empathy is a key combination of skills that allows us to drive change inside organisations.

We are all learning

With every new client and every new team, we need to go through the process of learning how to work with them in a way that gains trust and allows us to help them increase their design maturity. For this to be successful, we need allies who see the value design adds and will help spread the message. But while one approach may work for some people, it might be completely wrong for others, so it really is an ever-evolving learning process.

Maria Gomez, Director of Engineering at BCG Digital Ventures, has built many high-performing teams over the course of her career, and she told me her secret lies partly in one of her strengths being 'an includer'. While she is not the loudest voice in the room, her approach is to find out how everyone feels and understand their personalities.

When she's forming a team, she starts with a few 'storming sessions'* to get people feeling comfortable, so they're not afraid to participate, ask questions and give their opinions. There is always the danger that if you don't have the right leadership and direction, storming sessions can get out of control and become unproductive, particularly if you have a group of freelancers, which is common at BCG. Maria overcomes this risk by running a few sessions on different ways of working, testing the water with the team and then creating a 'working contract' that everyone signs at the start. She finds this helps the projects go 'super-smoothly'.

Putting these foundations in place might be seen as unnecessary and costly by some, but taking the time to get that alignment and agreement in place at the beginning creates a solid basis for the team and the project. As a design leader in these sessions, it's also important—especially if it's a digital delivery team—that you set the expectations and ways of working early. Depending on how deep and detailed you want to get, these could include:

- Everyone on the team helps to some degree with customer research and usability testing.
- Design, usability testing and user feedback will be continuous throughout delivery.
- Design will work one to two sprints/iterations ahead (depending on the project and sprint/iteration cycle).
- Design work will be visible and displayed on the team's planning wall, captured on a card in Jira, Miro, or similar.
- Research and findings from usability testing will be used to help make prioritisation decisions.

While you need to take the reins and be clear on your strategy for a project, an important part of learning is gaining feedback, taking criticism and listening to suggestions yourself. This allows us to grow as leaders and improve our approach. It is not a sign of failure—quite the reverse: the more we learn, the more we have in our 'toolkit' of ways to instil design inside the organisations we work with.

You will also find that, as a consultant, gaining feedback is a crucial component in backing up your argument for a promotion or steering your career in the right direction. Often, the people making decisions about your career don't know you and may have gathered their own feedback from people who also don't know you well or have heard things out of context. Having your own pool of feedback helps you to create a business case for why you are worth it.

---

* Based on Bruce W. Tuckman's *Four Stages of Group Development: Forming, Storming, Norming, Performing*. https://en.wikipedia.org/wiki/Tuckman%27s_stages_of_group_development

When you're the one giving feedback or critiquing someone's work, you don't want a lot of resistance—you want them to listen and consider your point. So, remember that it works the same in reverse: people need to trust that you can handle objections, so don't be the person who shoots down any feedback that doesn't go your way. Always make the effort to take criticism well because you will expect others to do the same.

So, to summarise . . .

While there are many traits that all leaders share, there are some that are unique to us as design leaders: our perpetual curiosity, our empathy and our need to solve problems and push our reasoning based on customer research and data, rather than our own agenda. Holding on to these fundamental design traits helps us drive forward as leaders.

Our constant need to improve the world we live and work in gives us an innate ability to inspire those around us, which can drive great change across teams and organisations. There's no need to be the stereotypical 'elitist designer'; we can still strive for the best and set high standards without being arrogant about our capabilities.

By understanding where our strengths lie and using an empathetic approach, we can build trust and relationships both within our consulting firm and externally with our clients. From this solid foundation, leading by example and being a positive guiding force, we can catapult ourselves to achieve great things for ourselves and everyone around us.

tw

TWO

design agency life vs large consultancy life

As a designer in a consultancy, you are often a consultant first and a designer second. Unlike in a design agency, consultancy life can feel like a merry-go-round of continuously justifying design's importance and taking teams and clients on a journey to understand the value design offers. In this chapter you will gain insights from design leaders on design agencies vs consultancies, their career pathways to design leadership and how to get ahead in a tech consultancy, as well as some observations from tech leaders on designers.

I n a design agency, you're surrounded by people who know what you do, and the entire business is driven by design from its core. In a large technology or business consultancy that has either acquired a design team or is trying to grow one organically, there is a learning curve for everyone. Many people will not know what a designer does or the value they add. And I'm not just talking about managers and leaders of the consultancy—it can also be the case with your own teams, as many developers and even some business analysts may never have worked with a designer before.

I come across this problem regularly. Older developers that have come from a more traditional IT background and been siloed by the organisations they work for have never had the influence level to work in a truly agile way, let alone experience adding continuous design to the mix. Sometimes it's just that the consultancy or client has always had a deep tech focus, and many younger developers, who are still in the early stages of their careers, have simply not had the opportunity to work with designers.

It's not that any of these people aren't willing to work with you and learn from you, they've just never had the chance. So it's your job as a consultant to understand who they are and how they operate, then break down these barriers.

In a design agency, clients come to you because you 'do design', whether that's advertising, branding, digital or print. Your job is relatively straightforward: to convince them you are the best in your field. Once you win the work, you'll solve the problem using processes similar to those you've used before. While there will still be deadlines and frustrations, as there are with any project, your team will know what they're doing and understand how the process works to enable you to get to the best solution for your client. And because the client has effectively outsourced the project to the design agency, there's no need to take the client and their team on the journey of understanding the nuances of design and how it works.

In a large consultancy, it's undoubtedly more complex and rather like having multiple clients. You have to start with the ones under your own roof, educating various people in the consultancy about design; then you have to educate the external clients. Many clients will come to the consultancy with what they think is a purely technical problem—they haven't yet considered the human impact and therefore the importance of the design element. So you'll need to take them on the journey of understanding the value of design, how designers and developers work together, how you might be embedded in their team, how you will do customer research and the value it adds. And, importantly, how this new way of working will provide the optimum solution to their problem.

It's very much sales and stakeholder management. Once you win the job, you will most likely be working from the client's office or remotely with people you have never worked with before, and you need to be prepared to meet some resistance. The word 'consultant' often stirs up images of sharply dressed, smooth-talking, overpriced advice givers who never get their hands dirty—which is far from the reality of a tech consultancy that exists to solve some of their clients' most complex problems! But as with every job, those who don't understand what you do and why you're there tend to stereotype.

So, to succeed as a design leader in this new environment requires a deep knowledge base of design's best practices and a relentless commitment to problem solving.

Common observations

Like all businesses, different consultancies have different approaches, structures and ways of solving their clients' problems, but you'll also face many common challenges when you move from a design agency to any consultancy. The design and tech leaders I spoke to have particularly noted the following:

The big picture

In an agency, you often have a limited view of the client, whereas in a consultancy you get to see the wider picture—the full strategy and, at a much deeper business level, why that particular problem needs to be solved.

Lauren Pleydell-Pearce, Executive Creative Director, PWC UK, had this to say:

> I'm now seeing behind the curtain. I've gone from being exposed only to this tiny bit of the conversation to really seeing the wider conversation about the strategy that's been going on for months. From a design perspective, it felt like we had such a limited view, but nevertheless, we had the right skillset to inform some of those strategic decisions. Now that we are getting into the meatier conversations, I don't think I ever realised how far away agency discussions were from the initial conversation.

Different justification

In a design agency, you sell a story and a concept; rarely are you required to give any significant business justification. In a consultancy, there's an entirely different level of scrutiny. You have to justify your work to the business or the person who lives and breathes it every day—it's *their* problem, and you have to convince them that *your* solution is the answer. You'll need to back up your design solution with data and know what the ROI is, and you could well be asked to justify how it contributes to the overall strategy and works with the existing tech constraints. This could be in a conversation with the cleint's product owner or the executive leaders who are not from the world of design or tech. Being anything other than well prepared isn't an option!

More influence

The nature of a consultancy allows you to get closer to your clients, which gives you a greater level of influence. You just don't get the opportunity to do this much in an agency unless you're the owner and/or have good relationships with the C-level execs. Even then, your focus as an agency is different—you might be focused on one specific area of design and therefore you don't want or need to know the overall business strategy. More influence does, however, come with more risk and more eyes on you, so a greater level of skill is required. A technical leader at one of the Top 4 consultancies offers:

> In a consultancy, you're forced to see the bigger picture. In an agency, you're in a silo, you're often focused and it's not uncommon to be unaware of what's driving the thing you're working on and where it fits into the client's organisation. You just know someone wants this thing done.

> In a consultancy, you have a broader view, you can trace back plans and see where everything aligns—but this has positive and negative effects. You have to be able to justify everything and how that relates to the bigger picture, whereas they're not really expecting you to do that in an agency, as long as your solution meets the stakeholder's objective.

There is no longer a defined career ceiling

Your career in an agency has a clear path, but there is a ceiling: once you reach Creative Director it doesn't go any higher unless you own the company. In a consultancy, because you have the breadth of capability and tend to have multiple areas of expertise, all areas are open to you. You can discover things you never realised you were interested in and build a career around one of those. A technical leader at one of the Top 4 consultancies had this to say:

> You learn tech, design and strategy at an agency and that's about it. I'm not trying to belittle it—I loved my time there—but at a consultancy the whole world opens up to you, and you have to be able to make a firm decision on what your direction is going to be.

Breadth over detail

In an agency, it's more important to know the details and to be more specialised, whereas as a design consultant, you need a breadth of skill and knowledge. You can still have a level of specialisation in a consultancy, but you'll have to deal with many different clients who will have a range of problems, so you've got to be able to adapt. Most importantly, it's not enough to simply be the best designer in the room; you need to be able to consult because you will be managing stakeholders, driving design and justifying design solutions to the business, speaking to departments you simply would never encounter as an agency designer.

Taking the client on the journey

In an agency, designers work together to create solutions that get presented to the client, along with a story to explain the approach and the reasoning behind it. But they don't have to justify their work process in the same way as a designer in a consultancy does.

As a consultant, when you have a new client, you need to build trust by taking them along on the design journey to help them understand what you're doing and why. You'll need to explain why and how you will conduct the research, why you need to test ideas with their users—even why you need access to their users at all. You're likely to be sat in the client's offices or, if remote, you will be working with a cross-functional team and attending stand-ups where you need to explain what you're working on.

You have a dollar sign on your head, so you need to justify both the need for you to be there and the value of the work you're doing. In an agency, you deliver the work; in a consultancy, you deliver and teach.

> " In an agency, you deliver the work; in a consultancy, you deliver and teach. "

> Design consultants have T-shaped skills: a breadth
> of business skills with deep design expertise.
>
> Jennifer Martin, Associate Partner, Asia Pacific
> Experience Design Leader, EY

Cooking with an audience

In an agency, you get to go away, work on your own and then come back with your idea, but in a consultancy, you need to be comfortable working in front of the client. Whatever you're 'cooking', you've got to stand in front of them and present the ingredients. So, if you're running workshops with the client and team, you'll need to be comfortable with jumping up and sketching on a wall.

Even now I find it hard to sketch in front of others. If it's the client, they usually don't worry about your drawing ability, although there does seem to be a misconception that all designers are amazing artists and have perfect handwriting. If I have the time to think, prepare and sketch out workshop material, I can make things neat, but in general my handwriting is appalling—'creative' but appalling. Interestingly, I've observed that developers tend to have neat handwriting, especially on sticky notes!

The 'wall' and the problems it causes

The following is from an interview with a technical leader at a Top 4 consultancy:

> I have learnt that good designers have good reasons why they do everything. Nothing happens by accident—they've poured over it and have the data to go with it. But if an agency isn't cross-functional and they don't all have the same briefing, when stuff is handed 'over the wall' to the tech team on the other side, they don't know why the design decisions have been made. And if they don't understand the purpose, they won't understand the importance of keeping the thing consistent. When you simply hand over to a third party, the danger for the project is that they may not have the same priorities, the context, or the design appreciation.

The reality is that some agencies and consultancies have cross-functional teams, and some hand their designs over the wall to another department, include a designer at the start but then remove them from the team for the build or delivery phase or hand it to a third party to build, and this choice of process can have a profound impact on the final result (see Figure 2.1). It can mean the difference between the design's being brought to life in a way that perfectly solves the problem or completely failing because the delivery team either can't build it or don't understand the requirements or priorities.

Some consultancies that have bought design agencies have failed to successfully integrate them and find a cross-functional way to work. That has resulted in the agency's being 'tacked on', which causes misalignments.

1 year of research was undertaken to understand the problem and gather insights from customers.

The business wanted to turn a complicated application process into a seamless and intuitve digital experience that was accessible for all. The existing process required users to gather information from various services to complete the application process.

External contracting company (UX Designer and developers) appointed to design and build the solution.

The solution was designed and tested on customers, and they loved it! The solution was designed to be fully integrated, enabling the process to be seamless from signup to completion. There was a clear navigation and stepper indicator, and customers could now gather the information required qucikly and easily.

The developers and product owner prioritised time and effort and ignored all the previous research and design phase, which they had been part of.

The business was sold on the solution, and a large budget was allocated to build it.

The developers used some components from the company's design system. If a component didn't exist, rather than custom building it, they would find something from a different library that required less effort to implement, regardless if it was intuitive or solved the problem.

The developers and product owner were left to make any decisions that arose.

The UX designer was removed from the delivery phase (not seen as needed for delivery).

The team changed the style of important elements, such as the stepper and main navigation, and moved them to the bottom of the screen because that was easier to build.

The product could not be launched to customers, wasting millions dollars.

The business had to start all over again with a new team. The code was in such a poor state they had to start from scratch; funding could now only be released in small amounts, taking the team over three years to build the solution for customers.

The final product was handed to an internal team to test on users. It failed spectacualry on every level—acessibility, interaction— and left the user confused with multiple redirects and confusing messaging.

Figure 2.1 Handing the design 'over the wall' can have disastrous results

If the agency doesn't have the full picture and doesn't properly understand the ROI and how to create something feasible, they will simply focus on designing the best possible vision and ideal solution. When it then gets handed over to the delivery team or the strategy team, they may well be confused and say it can't be built because either the technology doesn't exist or it can't be integrated with their systems. The designers have wasted their time and the consultancy has failed to create a solution at the first hurdle.

The structure that you as a DesignedUp leader need to ensure is cross-functional teams, where tech is included in the early conversations about design and there's no 'wall'. The individuals may not all sit in the same department, but they will be brought together as one team for projects. This approach enables multiple viewpoints and ideas to come together, highlights any possible technical constraints that need to be considered and gets everyone on the same page, working towards the same goal and aligned around the customer experience.

As Maria Gomez, Director of Engineering at BCG Digital Ventures, reflected during our interview:

> Nobody wants a 'design sandwich', where the designer hands the design over the wall, it gets built, then handed back, and the designer says, 'That's not what I wanted!'

Location, location

Some agencies specialise in a particular medium or industry and this shapes who they are as a business and therefore the designers they attract. With consultancies, the focus and specialism can often change, depending on the location of the offices. Because the work they do is more complex—whether it's strategy, business, tech or problem solving—coupled with the high fees and larger teams needed to solve these issues, they are often limited in the clients who have the means to work with them.

So, with different industries being more prominent in different locations, you could work for a multi-office consultancy that gets the majority of its work from the government in one city, then move to another office in another state or country and you get to work with some of the leading cool tech and product companies.

That's one of the advantages of working for a large consultancy and it's normal for people to move around offices and countries—the opportunity is often there if you want it. With the added bonus of remote working, if you are happy to be flexible when your working day starts you can take the opportunity without the travel.

Visibility = opportunity

When you're on the ground at the client's site, it makes it much easier to have visibility on how the company operates and spot opportunities where you can help them. This is harder in the remote world, and you will need to work harder on building your network and listening to comments made during zoom calls.

As a design leader, you will also have access to people who you might not get the opportunity to meet if you were in an agency and working in silo to the client. This collaborative and integrated way of working with the client, whether on-site or remotely, makes it easier for you to break down silos and embed design ways of working and methodologies across more than just your own team or department.

Having this wider view across an account and gaining deeper knowledge of a particular project could also help you to assess how other teams are performing. Getting to know people from different teams will help you understand what gaps they might have—what are you doing that they aren't? Is there a way you could collect this information and present it to the client to help them increase their design maturity and help you grow your influence across the account?

As you're on the ground with the client, consultancies will expect you to feed information back to them about any opportunities you can help them with. They'll also expect you to let them know about any risks you may have uncovered— you're their eyes and ears on the front line.

Where are my client's pain points? Is this something we can help solve?

And it's a win/win: you're there to help the client achieve their goals, so if you've found risks or identified a new way they could improve their offering, they will thank you for that and your consultancy will gain more work. You just need to make sure it's communicated in the right way.

Even though you may be on the ground working with the client, you won't necessarily know the politics within the organisation, and if you've come from an agency, delivering constructive feedback to them might seem like a sales job. You just need to put your designer hat on and look at it as you would a design problem: Where are my client's pain points? Is this something we can help solve?

Getting involved in sales

Some consultancies expect their more senior consultants to help with client pursuits. This is your opportunity to educate those involved about design, ensure the proposal includes design and isn't just focused on the technology or business problem, then question whether what the client is asking for is really the right solution to their problem. You can also help shape what the team looks like and ensure they put the right type of designers on the project.

Use your storytelling skills to tell the right story, and use your empathy skills to ensure it will resonate with the people you're presenting to. Show just how much value you can add at every stage through your design ability and natural leadership traits.

Working in the tech industry will require you to have some tech knowledge. You don't need to be able to write the technical requirements for a proposal, but you'll need to wear your tech, design and business hats to understand how the approach you're suggesting is going to work as a deliverable. If you're not a tech head, don't panic! I find that if I don't understand something, there is always someone who's willing to explain it in my language—you just need to ask.

How you get involved in sales within a design agency tends to depend on its size. In smaller agencies, jobs are often worked on by everyone: the creative director drives the vision, then art directors, designers, UX specialists, etc. all help to produce the final outcome. In larger agencies, the work may go straight to the specific client design team or digital team.

In a consultancy, the approach mainly depends on the structure of the consultancy and the value of the prize if the work is won. That said, the level of investment the consultancy is willing to make is not always directly related to the financial value; it can also be about how interesting the work is or whether it's considered a strategic investment—will the work open other doors? There are three key structures within which designers sit, each with different sales opportunities:

- **Dedicated teams.** Some large consultancies have dedicated internal teams who work on the larger pitches. They will also pull on resources from internal design agencies to make the presentation look good and ensure it conforms to their brand style.

- **Studio model.** Some larger consultancies have 'studios' where the designers sit, but they still work in cross-functional teams for delivery. Often the work is done using whoever is on the 'beach' or 'bench', along with a creative director to drive it. If you're a designer dedicated to a given project or account but you have some cycles or capacity, or if you're a designer who is currently on the bench, it is in your best interest to get involved in pitches and requests for proposals (RFPs).

  Luciana Albuquerque Gissing, Creative Director, Experience Design at Deloitte Digital, notes, 'They're selling the work you will have to do, so it's best to get involved so you can help shape that work.'

- **Dedicated pursuit team.** This works differently in each consultancy. If it's a large pitch that uses multiple departments within the consultancy—such as data analytics, development and design—they usually have a dedicated pursuit team within each specialism doing their bit. Other large consultancies will pull in specialists from the various areas to create one pursuit team. That team will pull everything together, conduct the pitches and respond to questions from the potential client, and everything goes through an approval process with people from legal, finance, delivery, etc.

  The downside of this dedicated pursuit team approach is that sometimes the best people to be on the team are on client projects and have to prepare pitches on top of their usual workload, so they may not be able to give it their full attention. Either that, or someone who may not have the full knowledge works on the pitch. Then, with the nature of consultancies being that current client work is given higher priority, if it's a longer pursuit in which there are multiple rounds, it's often not the same team seeing it through from start to finish. And multi-million-dollar pitches understandably have several stages, because a client isn't going to hand over that amount of money without doing their due diligence to select the right partner.

Although you tend to get assigned to sales pursuits based on your level of experience and availability, you can do things to nudge yourself towards the top of the list. In the same way that you need to build good relationships with the account handlers in a design agency, in consultancies you need to build good relationships with the sales team or those that decide who gets what consulting gig. The more they get to know and trust you, the more your name will be at the front of their mind when the interesting projects come in. Make sure you understand their motivations: if you can do something to help them win a certain account they've been trying to get—for instance, by putting together a strong proposal—you'll be remembered, and they can help influence when you need them to. Often it's *who* you know and not *what* you know.

Some consultancies have a strictly traditional hierarchy, and some have flat structures, making it easy to approach and pair with salespeople and other influencers. Others are structured so that individuals work towards specific goals for the year, meaning anything you ask other people to do and anything you want to do yourself will need to align with their and your respective goals. You need to find out early on how your consultancy works in order to figure out how you'll be able to grow.

Building these relationships isn't just about currying favour and getting the 'nice' projects. It gives you the opportunity to embed design into people's thinking and will help open the door for you to attend initial client meetings, where you can put the case for design at the forefront of the conversation. You'll be able to help the pursuit team understand design better, which is especially important if some of them have only sold solutions that focus heavily on technology, or they come from a different specialism, such as digital transformation or business analysis. They can learn from you and start repeating what you say in other conversations.

As consultants, we have the extra level of access within an organisation that agencies generally don't, and we can leverage this to make a greater impact and perhaps fundamentally change an organisation. Working closely with the sales team allows you to help them shape the right team for success; then, once you've won the work, you can start to influence how design works both within the team and more widely across the organisation.

It's also a great way for you to learn more about how to talk to consultancy clients and will give you a better understanding of technology. For example, being part of early pitches allowed me to understand how to explain the process of dealing with a legacy system and how you can use the 'Strangler Fig Application'* to slowly decommission the old system and bring customers onto the new platform. This little bit of knowledge really helped when I was talking to a potential client over the phone and he asked how we approached re-imagining legacy systems. I was able to explain the Strangler Fig approach and how we would work with them to determine the best approach. That initial conversation led to our having further conversations and later winning a significant piece of work..

Design agencies and consultancies often create concepts to win pitches; however, many organisations require you to respond to a rigid RFP put together by procurement departments. These are often not visually stimulating, and you have to sell your story mainly using words rather than images. Large RFPs tend to be complex and require a

---

* The Strangler Fig Application is a pattern for rewriting and replacing an existing and often important, system with a new, more modern, one that is able to perform the same functions as the original system as well as adding new features. Following this pattern means gradually replacing the old system by building the new one around its edges and growing around it until it fully strangles the original system. This approach contrasts with a big rewrite followed by a one-off cut-over. The most important reason to consider using the Strangler Fig over a big rewrite is to reduce risk. https://martinfowler.com/bliki/StranglerFigApplication.html

lot of detail: explaining your process, your reasoning and where you have done it before; what the ideal team looks like; how much it will cost to roll out the solution across several countries; how you will help teams understand the cultural differences between these countries and their customers; and how you will adapt the product to be relevant for each country.

While these are all interesting problems to solve, it can be a challenge for designers to express and illustrate their ideas as they would like when there's a prescribed way of responding. If you're lucky, an RFP will not prescribe a format, so although it will mean more work for you if you don't have an in-house design department, you'll be free to create something visually stimulating that tells the design story in the best possible way.

Instant expert

When an organisation brings in a consultancy, many people instantly view the consultants as experts and therefore expensive (but we won't get into that!), especially if the consultancy has a good reputation for delivering. As a design leader, this perception is beneficial because it gives you instant credibility, and many people will seek your advice, which gives you a great platform for championing how design and delivery should work within the organisation. The downside is that some people in the organisation might feel intimidated by you.

A few years ago, we were building a new platform for a client who already had a UX designer within their organisation.

> **The more they trust you, the more you'll be at front of mind for the interesting projects.**

Although her work didn't directly affect our project, once the new platform was built, it would affect the product she was working on. In addition, she seemed to keep herself to herself. So, to prevent her from feeling isolated or left out, we invited her to join us for coffee and lunch, which allowed us to build a bond and find out how she felt.

It turned out she was just as passionate as we were about the various products, but she was finding it hard to get her voice heard and have any impact, as she was the only designer in a large team of developers, BAs and QAs, with a team leader who didn't fully understand the meaning, function and value of design. She had also never been allowed to do any face-to-face customer research and testing, which frustrated her. For us it was different—we had set out our expectations with the client from the start on how design and delivery work as one cross-functional team—so we decided we would work together to enable design to be heard.

We invited her to our research sessions so that she could learn about the customers she was designing for and ask questions specific to her product, as they all formed part of the same ecosystem. This united front made her feel supported, helped her with her work and also perfectly demonstrated to the organisation how design and delivery work as one. The fact that we were respected as experts with instant credibility enabled us to dictate our own working processes and help one of the client's own employees develop as both a designer and a team member.

Being seen as the 'instant expert' also means you can't hide in the corner anymore and simply design great experiences. So, if your focus is on honing your design craft and you prefer to work in the magical and special design bubble, then the tech consultancy world is not for you. No matter your level of design, you will need to be able to set up and defend your decisions to a client, understand how to deal with conflict and politics within client organisations and learn how to de-scope design based on time and budgets for delivery. Essentially, you'll need to develop a lot of new skills and juggle a lot of new hats.

As a consultant, you get to work inside organisations across a variety of sectors, which will give you an insight into how different companies operate. With every new client, you'll get to help them embed design into their processes, meaning that, one by one, you are teaching all kinds of organisations to think differently. If it sounds powerful, that's because it is—as long as you remember that they are hiring you because you are a design expert, not an expert in their business. Your role is to see through the complexity that they can't get past. Being an expert in their business would blind you, prevent you from seeing the problems and stop you from asking the right questions.

It's a complex path to tread. You need to be an expert in your field, with an understanding and empathy for your client's business; you have to be confident and skilful, yet humble and willing to learn. A large portion of your job will involve doing things you haven't done before, getting to grips with loads of new acronyms, understanding legislative requirements and so on. You will regularly feel like 'the newbie'; you'll be painfully aware of your own ignorance, and you'll have to be prepared to ask all the silly questions in order to unpack the problem. Success as a consultant requires a deep knowledge base of design best practices and a relentless commitment to problem solving and excellence. As I said at the start of the book, it can be utterly exhausting, so when you get that instant credibility, use all the benefits it offers you wisely!

Eat, sleep, repeat

Organisations get consultants in when they can't do the work themselves, either from lack of expertise or because they simply don't have enough staff to complete the project. They often have complex problems that go beyond just designing a new product, so the work might extend to re-organising how they function as an organisation or helping them execute large digital transformation programmes—perhaps even helping them grow internationally. While the specific problems may differ, the challenges you face and ways in which you work to achieve solutions with and for your clients will often be similar.

Some organisations may already have design teams that you need to work with, and some of these teams might work quite differently to you. In my experience, many are siloed and don't work in cross-functional teams with an agile approach, meaning they often never get to speak to the people building the products. This requires you finding a common ground that works for everyone and possibly up-skilling them in being agile and cross-functional.

A lot of organisations are not familiar with how to use design to de-risk ideas, develop innovations or really be human centred in their approach. They want to be like the cutting-edge brands that eat design and tech for breakfast, but they don't really understand how to get there. They don't know what it means to be truly design and tech focused and the impact this will have, both on their organisational structure and on their own mindset. It's a lot for you to tackle, but you need to be prepared to do it time and again, with client after client.

With every client, you will need to find your design advocates, build your followers and not only bring them along on the design journey but also do the actual design work you're being paid to do. Advocates for design come in varying forms. I've had programme managers who absolutely love it and see the value design brings right away, which is great because they have real influence. I've also had more junior developers fall in love with design and the way it can help the work and decisions they're making. This younger generation are also great advocates because they are usually vocal among their peers and will share their knowledge and then take it with them as they grow.

Be prepared to feel like you're repeating the same stuff with every client and team you work with, particularly if the team is blended with client employees, so you're regularly working with people you haven't worked with before. You will often be parachuted into a task, a project or an industry without the skills, experience or any context, and you have to adapt quickly. It's like changing your job every few weeks, except your induction will be vastly shorter.

Even if you've worked in a particular industry before, there will always be new things —new technology, new stakeholders, new tools, new co-workers. On one hand, you're constantly going through the same motions; on the other, the landscape and its inhabitants are never the same. As a design consultant, the environment around you is constantly changing, and you have to adapt fast to survive.

Career paths

Designers are great at making up titles to express exactly what they do, and with more and more niches being developed inside the tech world, it can become confusing. We really don't make it easy for ourselves or for others to understand what our level is or what we really do. However, inside a traditional agency model, there is a clear career path: junior designer, senior designer, art director and creative director. Once you're a creative director, that's it.

Those who find the ceiling too limited within an agency tend to prefer the consulting approach, in which you can have a broad role and move across different disciplines within the consultancy or find your own niche and define your own path. In this world you get from consultant, to senior consultant, associate creative director, senior associate, senior manager, lead consultant, associate partner, principal consultant, director—the range of titles goes on . . .

> **Organisations that value design—and designers—have accurate role descriptions and relevant career paths.**
>
> Jennifer Martin, Associate Partner, Asia Pacific
> Experience Design Leader, EY

Your progress through this unknown landscape will depend on the consultancy you work for. Some will provide you with a coach, who will work with you and help you set goals. They will advocate for you at the end of the year and present the case for why you deserve a promotion or whatever it is you've been aiming for. They will also be responsible for passing on any feedback and helping you work through overcoming any negatives. Other consultancies might not have anything like these processes in place, or if they do, they might be far from a well-oiled machine.

Whatever the setup of the consultancy, you will need to be clear to yourself about who and what you want to be. In the consulting world, where your teams change and you don't have a specific manager or creative director responsible for you, people won't generally have a view on what you're doing and the value you're adding. That means you need to look for opportunities at every turn to show design leadership and get your voice heard. You'll need to work hard at building relationships with people across different specialisms and outside the design circle, and you'll also need to gather feedback regularly, even if you have a coach.

Proving yourself requires a lot of work, and it can be hard to keep the momentum going when you also have complex projects to deliver or you spend a lot of time on proposals. It can also be hard to show you can tick all the delivery boxes if you're not on billable client work for long periods. This comes back to whether your consultancy has defined or blended roles; with the latter you need to be across many things at one time, which can impact your performance.

Even in the large consultancies, your career is self-driven, and you'll need to overcome the 'employee' mindset. You need to decide on your passion, on what gives you that buzz, and push for that. If there is a gap in the consultancy you want to close, you'll need to use your influencing skills to define why and how you want to do it.

I, for one, have found it hard to define what I really want in my own career. I'm passionate about so many areas of design, and I strongly believe that if you're a designer at your core, one of your strengths is that you can adapt to multiple problems and mediums. In the tech consultancy world, you are put in many different situations with clients in different fields and technologies ranging from the norm to the experimental, and you constantly have to adapt as a designer. This can make defining or working in one chosen specialism hard—more so if the clients you get to work with don't require that specialist skill. So, while you should strive to carve out a specialism that you can excel at, make sure you don't lose your flexibility and willingness to learn.

If you're mentoring or coaching others within the consultancy, get them to dig deep and think really hard about what they want to do. Ask them: What would you like to do? Is there something you want to pursue? How can I help you achieve that aim? And if you're still trying to define your own path, ask yourself the same questions. What do you want to be known for? A technical leader at one of the Top 4 consultancies described it this way:

> You have to get out of the mindset that there will be guardrails around what you can and can't do. As soon as you change your mind to know that you can do anything in this broad set, it's amazing! You feel like you really are in charge of your own destiny. I find it a positive, but it's certainly different to an agency.

It's almost like you're an employee in a design agency but need a self-employed freelancer mindset when you're a consultant. I asked the tech leader quoted above how they had managed to shake off the employee mindset to define and shape their career within a consultancy and how they had convinced people to let them take that direction.

> I looked at what I had learnt in my career. I looked at what I could see coming up—trends—and what I believed would become important in the future. I looked for somewhere that had room for a point of view that wasn't currently represented well but was a passion I could build a career around. That set my path and defined my direction . . .

An Aussie in Blighty

Lauren Pleydell-Pearce went on quite an adventure to become an Executive Creative Director at PwC. She's an Australian who moved to the UK and I'm from the UK but moved to Australia, so when we spoke, it was interesting to compare cultural differences, particularly the funny little things you don't think about when you move—differences that exist even between countries that speak the same language. Says Lauren:

> I started as a visual designer in a small agency in Sydney, where you needed to be jack of all trades. We had a large client in the UK, so the agency decided to open an office there to serve our client better and they asked if I would go over to help set up the office and a team. I said yes before I realised what I was saying yes to! Within three weeks, I had sold everything I had in Sydney and landed in the UK not knowing anyone, which sounds totally insane looking back.

> The company decided not to invest money in the UK business and asked if I would go back, but I had just found a flat so I decided to stay. I fell back into freelancing and landed in an agency that was focused strongly on digital: e-commerce, large-scale website builds and creative campaigns. I worked with a range of clients, but the highlight for me was pitching and winning Audi and going on to develop their digital design system, art directing the car photography and learning a huge amount on the way.

> After that, I felt I needed a change and realised I hadn't yet explored the land of design in London. I was given an opportunity to establish a creative start-up and help form a new team. I ended up being there for four years, and it was the first time I had the chance to shape a team properly. I got to look at the structure of it and decide what I wanted to put in place to run the team—the tools, the methodology, the culture—and then I could start to look at team performance.

> I was young, almost too young to be doing that. Looking back, it was a really sharp

No one just says, 'Yep, that's good'. They ask: 'What's the ROI, the size of this opportunity, the size of the market, what proportion of the market do you think you could own, is this worth putting our resources into . . . ?' It's a constant justification.

You know, I read something that really stuck with me: 'Find something you're really good at and find another thing you have proficiency in, combine the two together and occupy that space. One of those things should be something others find difficult or that you've seen them struggle with; then you're not going to be constantly competing to try and do it. Play to your strengths'.

learning curve. It was successful, but I think I was lucky in a lot of ways because I'd found the right people to help me.

With a lot of life lessons under my belt, I moved to WundermanThompson to be one of their Creative Directors, which was a really big step for me. I focused on brand-led digital design, specifically product design, supporting the creation of the Customer Experience team and bringing on new talent to further grow out our capability in this space.

To be honest, the role at PwC came out of the blue. I like doing a lot of different things, and I'd often had a crisis of identity as a designer until it occurred to me that I actually like solving problems. If you have a strategic problem, I like to come up with a design solution, whether it's an app or an experience, and the PwC role would give me the chance to tackle some complex social and strategic challenges at a level I would never be exposed to in an agency.

It also gave me the opportunity to build my team from scratch. I knew it was going to be difficult, but it was like the next evolution: I'd done it in the smaller start-up, then within an agency structure and now I would be doing it within a larger consultancy structure. There are around 3,600 people in the London office alone, so it gave me a chance to make a real difference.

Previously, there had been moments where my team would have diligently created what we knew was the right thing for the end consumer, but without a view into the organisation, we would be unaware that there were such deep silos inside. The client would be excited about the potential but realise it could go nowhere because what we were proposing would completely change the organisation and its structure.

Being sat inside a construct like PwC, where I now have the people around me to make those kinds of complete organisational changes happen, is quite a powerful thing.

Creating a vision for your career

Your career may change as you progress and are exposed to more of what the consultancy world has to offer, but the sooner you can form a clear vision that has substance and reasoning behind it, the sooner you'll be able to get started on a meaningful path. So:

- Gather feedback from those around you, including clients. They might point out skills you didn't realise you had.
- Look back on past projects, and write a list of what you liked and didn't like.
- Create a vision of where you'd like to be in the future—think five to ten years ahead.
- What is your personal 'brand'—what are you passionate about?

Once you have your research and vision, start talking to those who can influence your career path or advise on any gaps you have and how best to fill them. If your company has a mentoring programme, ask how you can participate; if this isn't something they offer, find a mentor yourself—someone inside or outside your organisation who's achieved the kind of success you'd like to emulate and whom you respect. Mentoring focuses on you as a whole, supporting you and helping you grow both personally and professionally, and it tends to be a long-term relationship.

Evan Bottcher (formerly Tech Director at Thoughtworks and now Head of Architecture MYOB) says his biggest tool is his network of mentors, all of whom are inside the organisations he worked for. Over the years he's built this external network that consists of what he defines as 'sponsors'—people who can open a door for him. He meets with some of them on a regular basis, and others are more ad hoc.

The other option that some people prefer—and many have in addition to a mentor—is a coach. Coaching is generally business oriented, with a focus on helping you achieve a particular task and a specific agenda. The big difference between the two is that a mentor has been there and got the t-shirt, whereas a coach can simply excel at practical processes—you could think of it as 'counselling' versus 'training'. What they have in common is that both are there to help you be the best you can be. Following is a comment by a technical leader at one of the Top 4 consultancies

> It takes less effort to become exceptional in an area you are already strong in than it does to become strong in an area you are weak in. The world rewards the exceptional over basic competence.

When Lauren Pleydell-Pearce joined PwC, one of the challenges she set out to solve for her design team was to ensure they were recognised and rewarded for their specialist experience whilst encouraging them each to develop and grow beyond what they knew:

> We have performance by grade, and you have your yearly objectives that a career coach works with you to define. There is then a panel where you present your business

case for what you have achieved throughout the year, stating what you did above and beyond your goals. You are then measured against everyone else in your grade.

The problem this creates is that a visual designer is being compared against a service designer or copywriter, for example, when these are totally different jobs and skillsets. It was really hard for people to get reward and recognition in their development, which was creating generalist rather than specialist behaviour. To solve this problem, I defined career paths across the team. Now we have 'soft skills', such as leadership, specialist, communications, and then the specialist deep skill pillar.

Every leader has a different approach to how they are going to achieve their vision. Some plan the journey and work on influencing those who can help them, like Maria Gomez. 'I had aspirations of where I wanted to go, and I influenced people with more power. I always think about the long-term and how I am going to get there'. Others, like the technical leader at one of the Top 4 consultancies, look for niches they can own and have a passion for, and then they put a business case forward to allow them to get there. One observation I made while interviewing people is that the ones who plan and put business cases together tend to be more on the tech side, whereas the more creative leaders tend to see an opportunity and take it—they're comfortable having an adventure, taking risks and solving problems as they go. There is no right or wrong way, it's whatever works for you, but always be open to changing your approach as your career develops. Joshua Stehr of Medium.com had this to say:

The best consultants are not experts. They're the best because they can apply themselves to any problem, in any sector, and take a step back and see it from a new perspective. They see beyond the complexities of the existing situation and ask questions that nobody thought of or were considered too obvious. Not being an expert is a strength, but it's nerve-racking.

Working agile

agile *adjective* (management)

Used for describing ways of planning and doing work in which it is understood that making changes as they are needed is an important part of the job.
(Cambridge Dictionary)

Although many software delivery teams adopt an agile methodology, many designers, even those creating digital products, have not worked in a fully agile way or in an embedded team. They still design and test prototypes and iterate, but some do this without involving developers, quality analysts or business analysts. To add to this, as a consultant you may also find that although many clients have teams working in an agile way, these are often teams of developers. They don't know how

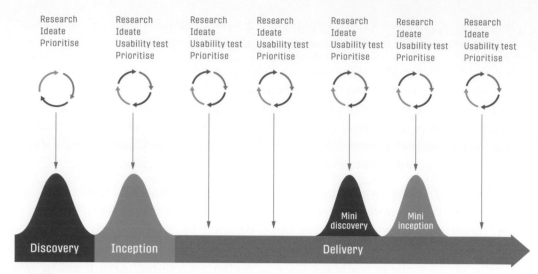

Figure 2.2 Throughout the lifecycle of the digital experience or product, the cross-functional team work together, continually testing the experience and ideas with users, then prioritise and build it.

the design process integrates and are sometimes concerned that adding design may slow them up.

In reality, embedding designers in delivery teams or working as dual-track cross-functional teams (if the organisation is willing to invest) gives you a number of diverse ways of solving a problem and enables you to continually bring user feedback into the delivery phase. This ensures the solution resonates with users, the right problem is being solved and that it can be built, greatly reducing the risks for the organisation. So, DesignedUp leaders need to explain exactly how design integrates and is able to bring in continuous customer feedback loops to help with prioritisation and building the right thing that will resonate with customers. (See Figure 2.2.)

Design leadership therefore requires a great deal of effort because you need to communicate your view and vision to an audience who might be unfamiliar with what a designer does. Not everyone will understand why design matters or why you need to test the solution on users. Some are just interested in writing great code and working in the back end, so you've got to find advocates who can help you break down these barriers. On the odd occasion, you may also have people on your team who are not designers but who disagree with you and believe they know better.

Setting expectations early as a design leader can eliminate many issues. Here are a few methods that I use regularly to facilitate an agile working environment:

- Set the expectation that you will need access to real customers for testing. Do this in the first client conversations, before a contract has even been signed.

- Again, at the outset, explain how you work as a designer. If you're going to propose pairing with developers and working in cross-functional teams, set that expectation early to avoid resistance.
- Use the product vision as your team's 'north star'.
- Collaborate as a team on design principles at the earliest stage. This will help when making design and tech decisions later on during delivery.
- When defining the team's way of working, set the expectation that you require everyone on the team to get involved in user research and testing, even if they are just observing. This is vital to ensure they all have a customer mindset—people have more empathy for users when they hear and observe their frustrations first hand.

You may also find yourself as the only designer on a delivery team. This might be alien to you, and many designers coming into the consulting world worry about not having other designers to bounce ideas off. However, while the rest of the team may not understand your design language, you'll be surrounded by people who are problem solvers—developers and BAs love solving problems just as much as designers do. They will bring different perspectives and ideas that will only enrich the final solution. You just need to ensure the solution remains human centred and doesn't turn into something that's highly technical but unusable. This will come out in usability testing.

Having cross-functional agile delivery teams is the only way to deliver solutions that work in a timely and cost-efficient way, and it always astounds me that so many delivery teams still have no idea about working agile with designers being embedded. Instead, they either do the design work up front or treat it as pretty garnish at the end!

Consultants are not given much time to understand the lay of the land when they get onsite with a client; they're expensive and need to deliver as quickly as possible, so if they want to do great work and impress and retain the client, the dynamic of the team is critical.

The success and performance of any team, in any industry, is defined by the people within it. The entire team needs to have each others' backs, be respectful and align to the same vision. No matter how talented each individual might be, if they cannot work as a team it will be a disaster. This is of particular importance for consultancies when they're deciding who to put on which client project—they need to weigh all the different skills and personalities if they want to create high-performing teams. Great teams are composed of individual contributors with complementary skills who think 'we', not 'me'.

Who is the customer?

Clients bring in consultancies when something isn't working, they don't have the right skillsets, or they can't increase their headcount of permanent staff. Using consultants gives them the flexibility they need as they grow.

The clients you will work with will be at varying stages of design maturity and capability. Some won't even know what the pain points of their customers are, due to a lack of data; some will have clunky processes for designing and building experiences; others will have inhouse design teams that may be embedded or not—and then there will be those that have it all figured out and just need help nudging the needle a little further.

They may be a successful technology brand with designers already in their ranks but still see themselves as a tech company, rather than a digital product company. In this case, you'll usually find design and tech are not working in unison, and designers have been siloed.

As a consultant, you could find yourself assigned to any of these clients, and your job will be to take them from wherever they currently are to where they need to go. In my experience, no matter what their design maturity, there will always be gaps and opportunities for you to prove your value.

Building trust with clients will help you gain the access you need to their customers and their data. This is critical, because every problem that needs solving will require you to gain a clear understanding of who their customers are and what opportunities there are to improve the customer experience. Understandably, some clients will not be comfortable unleashing a consultant they don't know on their precious, longstanding customers, so you'll have to seek out the people that can give you those insights, which will require a lot of one-on-one conversations.

One of the easiest ways to gain initial insights and get the wider team and stakeholders to understand customer pain points is to ensure customer-focused people are involved in product discovery workshops. It gives them a reason to be excited about the changes that need to be made and makes them feel part of the journey. There's also an element of education, so that it's not just, 'Here are the changes', but 'Here's why we're changing and how it will improve the customer experience'.

If you can position yourself so that you're involved in the sales and pitch process, you can explain to the client at the outset why having early access to customers is vital to successfully solving their problem. Demonstrate how you've done it in the past with anecdotal evidence—people love stories, and it's usually the thing they walk away remembering. Setting the expectation early will make accessing customers much easier once the work starts.

A tech perspective . . .

. . . on designers

Some consultancies will be coming from a tech-heavy history, and in the same way as we designers are figuring out how tech processes fit with how we work, they are learning how design fits in terms of its processes, methods, varying roles and types of designers.

I'm lucky that the majority of tech people I've worked with are collaborative. I've also had a few who have thrown their toys out of the pram and refused to play. But what do they think about us? Heads of technology, technical directors and tech principals I spoke to revealed some of the common traits they see and admire in designers:

Ability to unpick a problem. Designers need to see and hear from the people using the software so they can clarify what the business needs and create a better solution to meet these needs. They are great at getting to the root of the problem and aligning with the business needs.

Challenge our thinking. Designers push to do small experiments to test ideas, and they also question whether a tech fix is what's really needed at all. This brings a new perspective and challenges many people's go-to solutions.

Communicating the WHY. Some leaders think they need a blog or a newsletter to communicate; however, communicating the WHY is more important. Designers are good at getting everyone aligned and understanding why they are doing what they are doing.

Flexibility. Designers understand what restrictions may arise, and they're able to accept suggestions from non-designers. They don't mind if an idea isn't their own or if it came from a non-designer—what's important is that the right solution is found that solves the problem.

Curiosity. Design leaders are always curious and want to learn about the world and things outside design. This helps bring different perspectives and ideas to their work.

As leaders, we shouldn't shy away from questioning the 'why', challenging other people's thinking, taking a different view and listening to other perspectives. It's clearly a trait that others admire in us, and we must make sure we use it to build team relationships, influence and change the status quo.

. . . on the differences between the sexes

It was also interesting speaking to technical leaders of both sexes about the uncomfortable subject of male vs female leaders. We had some great conversations, and some common themes arose regarding female leaders across all disciplines.

Everyone agreed that women are more empathetic. We have a natural ability to nurture others and pick up on body language and tone of voice. Because of this, we're comfortable digging deeper to understand more fully, which makes us great problem solvers and team builders. However, this can sometimes result in our being pushed into a more managerial role, rather than having our creative side harnessed. One female design leader observed: 'The beautiful UI work is mainly done by men, the UX and managerial work is mainly conducted by females. I think this is because women tend to be seen as more caring and concerned with how their team are doing'. This from a technical leader at one of the Top 4 consultancies:

This is a gross generalisation, but I have found my female colleagues to be more humble, collaborative, willing to listen and understand that they don't have all the answers. Men have a lot of elitism, and the commercial world—not just consulting—rewards strong opinions. However, anyone, regardless of gender, who can take a bit of push back and keep going is eventually going to succeed.

> **Anyone, regardless of gender, who can take a bit of push back and keep going is eventually going to succeed.**

One common observation from the tech leaders I spoke with was that women who lack the confidence to push ahead with an idea tend to look inwards, whereas most men's natural dominance enables them to simply carry on regardless of how they might feel inside. Another observation was that many women feel uncomfortable trying to find common ground with the men on their teams—for instance, they don't feel as though they can contribute to a conversation about football.

Now, I know that's not true of all women—I have many friends who are passionate about their sports!—however, it's clear that we need to find different ways to overcome our fears, reduce Imposter Syndrome and find common ground for men and women to build comfortable and mutually beneficial working relationships. Sometimes certain things will work and other times they won't, so you need a few options in your bag.

Maria Gomez tells this story:

> I worked for an online betting company after University. It was a toxic environment. They were really surprised a woman wanted to be a tech lead. How can you flourish in that

environment? I was like, 'I'm out of here'. I had six females in my class and only two now work in the tech industry.

You need to find common ground with those you work with, and running ice breakers in workshops is a good way to find out more about people's interests. Before I had family commitments, it was much easier to go to drinks after work with the team, which I always appreciated as a great opportunity to bond. Now I use coffee/hot choc and lunch to catch up with some people and leverage my love of fitness to foster other connections.

Some business parks have free exercise classes over lunch, and I've found attending these has helped build relationships. I met the head of tech at one of our clients there one lunchtime—it turned out we both like running and cycling, so a few of us started to go running at lunch. At the other end of the spectrum, I was once working with a client who had employed a product owner who was 'old school', and I had been warned he wasn't the easiest person to get along with. I knew he had a deep history in the gaming industry, so even though I'm not a gamer myself, one day in the kitchen I asked him about his background.

It turned out he was really passionate about gaming and went on to tell me about the various articles he'd written. I think he appreciated that I'd made the effort, but it still didn't stop him from being extremely sexist towards the women on the team, including me. You can't win them all!

Bridging the gap

While there are common approaches we can adopt to reduce the gap between design and other disciplines once we're working together, the first thing we must do as consultants —before the project has even started—is get the client on board with our approach.

Kevin Yeung, Head of Data Platform at 3P Learning, had a bad experience with a well-known problem-solving design company. He likens the project to a watermelon (green on the outside, suggesting everything is running to schedule, but red on the inside, where challenges or obstacles are being overlooked):

> The client was a typical requirement-driven waterfall shop where every requirement was analysed and written down. During the project, once the requirements were understood to a certain degree, the designers felt there was no need to be with the dev team to iterate. They simply took the meeting notes back to the office and created hi-fi wireframes and prototypes.
>
> When the prototypes and interactions were unveiled to us and the client, it caused the scope of the project to significantly increase. This was because our team were now expected by the client to meet the new requirements, which meant we had to cater to the asynchronous endpoints, data validations (because it all happens in

the browser) and state persistence (if the browser crashes, we needed to remember where the user was).

If the designers had sat with us and talked through what they had in mind, we could have let them know the tech constraints. The client could have then decided how to spend the time and money to create value. Instead, it was 'required' of us to build the fancy design, with the assumption that value is automatically achieved without evidence.

The client was risk averse and saw our system as another IT project to be delivered on time and within budget. This put huge pressure on the development team to deliver. If more time had been spent getting the agreement right, establishing the correct expectations with the client, testing an idea, doing the research, getting feedback and trying different things, it could have been a different story.

Getting the foundations right sets the team up for success; then it's about defining how you want to work. For example, if it's a complex problem or a new product idea, you might say you need more time at the start to understand the problem and test ideas. If you're at an agency, you might want to spend some time onsite with the team and some time offsite to think and create in a space you're comfortable with. Whatever you decide, find an approach that works for the team and that everyone agrees on. The most important thing is having alignment and ensuring you're all heading towards the same goal.

The type of consultancy and its focus will determine what other skills you might need to bring on board or learn in order to bridge the gap. For instance, some consultancies focus more on delivery, and therefore excelling in this area can give you more credibility.

Mike Mason commented in one of our interviews:

I can see many advantages of design and tech working together. It shortens the feedback loop, designers get to understand tech constraints and the collaboration brings out new ideas. In the same vein is having a customer or a good customer proxy on the team. It means you can avoid going down the wrong path and wasting an afternoon, a day or a week doing something that you then need to undo. The cost of those little mistakes, even if you catch them, adds up and impacts the project . . .

I feel like technologists can learn at least a little bit about design; part of that collaboration process means they will get better and better at mostly doing the right thing once the groundwork is laid. That reduces the load on the design team because they're not answering easy questions all the time and can spend their time on more complex, higher value stuff.

I just don't see a disadvantage. Maybe there are scenarios where you need to consider several options and you want the design team to go away and think deeply about something. Maybe then it does make sense to have some separation, but that would be for some quite specific stuff.

Our ability as design leaders to be empathetic, solve problems and be curious can really help us bridge this gap between design and tech. It enables us to lead cross-functional teams effectively, using our empathy and vision to create synergies between the BAs and tech leads and to ensure we're all working towards solving the problem, keeping the customer as our central focus. This allows us to create a cohesive team environment in which creativity and ideas can spawn.

> **If we don't have a designer on the team, we'll just get the same thing we had before.**
>
> Project Manager, government organisation

So, to summarise . . .

Design agency life offers the security blanket of being surrounded by other creatives who all 'get' each other. There is also a certain buzz that you only find within an agency—an optimism that anything is possible—and your career path is well defined, albeit with a ceiling. You can specialise and spend all day doing design if that's what makes your heart sing. However, you're unlikely to be exposed to the wider issues of an organisation or have visibility on where your solutions fit within their strategy. Unless you're the creative director or owner of the agency, you may never get to meet or speak to the client directly about your idea.

On the other side, while a consultancy can certainly open up your world to a wealth of opportunities, you will be first and foremost a consultant and a designer second—and not everyone is made of consulting or leadership material. Some consultancies are still grappling with how to help designers progress and carve a career path, which can often mean designers are left in a state of 'limbo', unsure what their future might look like. The consulting industry needs you to constantly eat, sleep and repeat, taking every new client on the journey of design, helping them increase their design maturity and teaching every new team you work with how design functions and the benefits of being customer centric. Different people, same processes.

Being the glue between disciplines, working every day to close the tech and design gap and needing endless energy to complete the same journey with every new client might sound as though it's not much fun. But I can testify to the fact that being a DesignedUp leader in a consultancy could be the role of your life—if you're prepared to roll up your sleeves, step into the unknown and tolerate (even thrive on) being uncomfortable. Remember that your ability to unpick a problem, challenge the thinking of both the client and your team, stay flexible and be constantly curious are all traits that technologists respect and admire in design leaders. So step up and don't stop doing what you do best.

th

ree

design leader in an agile consultancy world

Working in a true agile environment is similar to the iterative design process, but there can be added challenges, such as a lack of thinking space and time to contemplate designs and possible trade-offs. And many designers don't realise that working in a tech consultancy doesn't mean they will always be working on cutting-edge technology and solutions. This chapter will focus on bringing your past with you, learning to let go, the similarities between designers and developers and why unicorns don't exist.

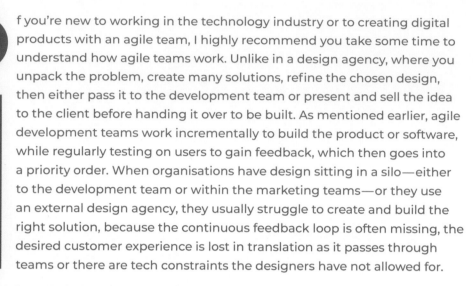

f you're new to working in the technology industry or to creating digital products with an agile team, I highly recommend you take some time to understand how agile teams work. Unlike in a design agency, where you unpack the problem, create many solutions, refine the chosen design, then either pass it to the development team or present and sell the idea to the client before handing it over to be built. As mentioned earlier, agile development teams work incrementally to build the product or software, while regularly testing on users to gain feedback, which then goes into a priority order. When organisations have design sitting in a silo—either to the development team or within the marketing teams—or they use an external design agency, they usually struggle to create and build the right solution, because the continuous feedback loop is often missing, the desired customer experience is lost in translation as it passes through teams or there are tech constraints the designers have not allowed for.

I have witnessed all these set-ups failing on every level within both medium-sized businesses and large organisations. Fundamentally, when the designers are disconnected from the technical requirements and engineers are left out of the design ideation process, it tends to lead to ideas that can't be built, that are built incorrectly or that are simply too expensive to build (as shown in Figure 2.1 on page 65). There should be a north star that everyone is aiming for—the designers' vision of what the product could be to solve the customer's problem—and the journey towards the star should be flexible to allow for new information from customers and advances in technology to shape and create the product over time.

Having design and tech working side by side saves a lot of time and allows design decisions to be made on the spot and prevents the waste of millions of dollars as described earlier. It also enables developers to be creative and bring their ideas to the table.

There are a whole host of issues that can arise, that require designers, developers and business analysts to work together to solve as the product is being developed. These could be small issues with designing for different operating systems—for instance, designing and building for iOS and Android apps using React Native® or even Xamarin®, where it's one code base and a multitude of devices to cater for. Or, if you're building a native app, it could be something more complex, where a problem arises due to 'spiking' a tech solution, using an API that doesn't perform as expected, or the screen reader needs adjusting based on feedback after conducting usability testing and you need to either collaborate to get it to work or take the decision to abandon it.

It's a very different world to work in. You need to be okay with ambiguity and with the idea that the first release will not have everything you envision or every bit of functionality. You'll need to understand tech and business constraints and work closely with business analysts at the same time as designing and driving human-centred design thinking across both the team and the entire organisation. It will be your job as a DesignedUp leader to show everyone the way.

Don't forget where you've come from

Even if you've come from a more traditional design agency, or your past consultancy did things very differently, don't think you need to forget everything and just adopt your current company's ways of doing things. Many developers and business analysts have never worked with designers before, and a lot of them will not fully appreciate what you do or the value you bring until they experience it. If you want to be a DesignedUp leader, you'll need to show people the way and lean on your past experiences to bring something new to the team. Your ideas might not solve every problem, but you won't know unless you try, so have faith in yourself and give it a go.

A couple of years ago, I was supporting one of our consultant-level designers who had moved over from the States. She had worked with some great companies but didn't have the consulting skills, and although we'd built up a great relationship, she was very much under the impression that she had to do her work 'the Thoughtworks way'. During one of our check-ins, she explained an approach she had used in her previous agency that she wanted to take with a client project. I thought her proposal was a great idea and reassured her that it was fine to try it out—even if it didn't work, there would be no negative impact on the project. She appreciated my support, and it gave her the confidence that she could try things going forward.

While every consultancy has their own framework for how they work, you'll find it's rarely set in stone. Remember that you were hired because of what you know, so bring your wealth of experience to the table, build on it and teach others through your skills and experience.

Thinking beyond your assigned role

As a DesignedUp leader, you need to think beyond just the design of the product or service; you've got to think about it from the very start of the design process all the way to it's being used by people in the real world. Once it's out there, you then need to ensure it stays relevant and valuable, both to users and to the organisation.

How will the business determine if it's a success or not? Digital products or services need constant evolution until they are decommissioned, which requires budgets to be continuously assigned, so what does the business need to see in order to keep funding the product or service? How will the product or service actually get out into the world? Has anybody thought about how customers will find the product or first discover the service? Has marketing been engaged early on? All this might sound pretty obvious, but you'd be surprised at how even some of the largest companies haven't thought everything through or fail to engage the right teams or departments early on.

Case study: Major bank 'sharing bills' feature

One of our major bank clients had a mobile app that was heavily used by their customers, but the existing target market for the bank focused on an older demographic. During an internal hackathon, they conceived the concept of creating a feature within the existing banking app to solve the issue of friends sharing the cost of bills—something younger people do on a regular basis, according to research. The new feature would allow users to send texts to their friends, telling them how much they owed and giving their bank details, along with a unique reference number that could be used to track when payment had been made. This concept was seen as something that solved a problem for customers, would allow the bank to target a new, younger audience, and would be a feature that no other bank was offering at the time.

The concept was successfully pitched at an internal investor day, and the team were given a small budget to explore the idea further. Once this phase was complete, it was handed to the mobile app team, where I was consulting. The new feature couldn't simply be added within the existing app's code base like the business and creators thought, and there were still a lot of areas we needed to help them solve in terms of the user experience, functionality and technology—all of which had to be achieved within a short time and limited budget.

Get it out, then get it right

Leaning on my past experience of running a full-service design agency and knowing how common it is for delivery teams to just focus on getting the work done, rather than thinking about how it's going to get out into the world, I was concerned that we were about to add a feature to our well-respected app that hadn't been tested with customers. Thanks to the connections I'd made, I discovered early on that the marketing department had unexpectedly been given a large budget to promote and market the new feature. Even when the app first launched, it hadn't received anything like this level of marketing funding.

In my eyes, this was a huge risk. If the client invested in a huge marketing campaign and then it turned out the feature wasn't something users wanted or it wasn't intuitive enough to use, it could result in a backlash against the brand. The demographic they were targeting wouldn't be afraid to share their views on social media, which could easily prevent the brand from gaining the trust it needed to entice new customers.

Initially, the business wanted to go straight to launch, to tap into the new target market and grow their market share. I raised my concerns within the team and then, together with the BA and tech lead, put together a proposal recommending a new plan of action. We suggested extending the deadline and launching an MVP (minimum viable product) to gather quick feedback before announcing that we'd created this great new feature. We presented this to our stakeholder, who had a lot of influence within the organisation, and it resulted in our being given more time to test the concept before the official launch.

Having built a successful agile, continuous design and delivery team, we were able to quickly and easily get a lightweight version of the feature into the app and test it with real users in a real-life situation. Taking the 'get it out, then get it right' approach allowed us to learn quickly from customers, greatly reducing the risk of launching something customers didn't actually want and damaging the brand's reputation.

Improving the MVP ready for official launch. Within a few hours of launching the MVP, we could see people using the feature and what they were splitting bills for. The feedback confirmed it was something they wanted and would use, but it also showed that our initial planned prioritisation of functionality was incorrect. Based on customer feedback, we were able to re-order the prioritisation and build a solution that satisfied what was important to them.

Taking the idea to market. Sharing with the marketing team what we had learnt from customers during the MVP phase helped drive the messaging for their campaign. Our collaborative approach meant we were able to work together on timelines and deadlines for a successful launch. Not only was the brand able to tap into a new customer segment, but taking a customer-centred approach resulted in the feature's winning multiple user experience awards.

I was just days into joining Thoughtworks when I was put on this major bank account, and my official assigned role was purely as an experience designer, with a remit to continue on from the previous designer and work on upcoming features and stories. It was seen as a 'safe project' to help me get into the agile way of working and an opportunity for Thoughtworks to assess my capabilities—however, 'safe' has never been my style! If I see a problem, I will always try and solve it—that's the mindset you need to have as a DesignedUp leader.

Using the knowledge you've built up over the years, looking at the wider picture and the full end-to-end life cycle and having the confidence to point out glaring gaps will help demonstrate your leadership. Don't be afraid to be different—as long as you can present the problem with potential solutions, backed up with solid reasoning, speaking up can only work in your favour. Even if the answer is 'no', for whatever reason, the fact that you've tried is worth a lot.

> **"Working agile allows you to pivot quickly and react to changes or new discoveries . . . "**

When agile meets obstacles

While working agile allows you to pivot quickly and react to changes or new discoveries, there will always be technology and business constraints, as well as unforeseen discoveries, that will need to be worked around. So, working as a designer in the tech industry often requires balancing your ideals of a user experience with these constraints—and sometimes you'll have to accept that something simply can't be changed.

Perhaps it will take too long or be too costly, and in some cases, past tech decisions are too far embedded in the organisation, and any change in direction would require a huge investment or redirecting resources away from innovation.

Being stuck with the inability to change quickly doesn't sound very agile, because agile allows you to test, learn and build incrementally. But you'll often find yourself helping a company to reimagine a legacy system that comes with baggage from the past that impacts your vision and the user experience. Not every project is greenfields, where you get to start with a clean slate; often the larger and more established the organisation, the more baggage there is that needs to be considered.

The problems may not even come from legacy software; perhaps, beneath the surface, fairly new products, services or APIs simply haven't been thought through to the user experience, or the organisation has selected a product without considering whether it will best solve the problem.

We were implementing a 'Create Account' flow, which should have been fairly straightforward, even with the various security tokens it needed to handle. From a user point of view, it should have been easy and seamless. The head of IT was a fan of a particular cloud platform provider, and many of their products and services were well embedded in the organisation, so it had already been selected as the tool of choice prior to our starting.

We soon discovered that one of their services didn't provide a very user-friendly experience. Once the user had entered their details, they would receive an email to activate the account, which was quite common; however, the email looked like spam, and once the user clicked the link to activate the account, instead of being taken to the login screen, they were essentially directed to a 'dead end' page and would have to navigate themselves to the login tab. The first impressions of using a product really count, and having a smooth, simple 'Create an Account' experience should be a given with any new digital product.

I walked through the problem from a user's perspective with the head of IT, explaining how it wouldn't look good for their brand when they launched the new product. Although he was a huge advocate for this particular company's software from a technical perspective, he could now see the issue it would cause customers—and that was something he hadn't considered before, simply because they had never taken a customer-centric approach to developing products. Previously, the tech team had been given direction from marketing or the customer engagement team on what needed to be built—they'd never had someone look at the entire user flow and consider both tech and the user experience. He was eager to help with the issue and arranged for us to meet with the provider's team to find a solution.

They were very understanding; however, they had a backlog of improvements to make and couldn't give a timeframe for resolving our issue. It would be too risky to use their new beta version, so they suggested we use a lambda as a workaround in the meantime. I was very disappointed. I understood they had a backlog, but I was expecting more from a company as large as this. How could they leave a user with a dead end?

I spoke to our tech lead about the possibility of using a lambda; unfortunately, it was going to be hard to know how much effort would be needed to do so. Given our timeline and budget, we couldn't afford to spend the time trying to fix it—we needed to focus on higher-priority customer needs. And we couldn't swap to another provider because the service was far too ingrained in the organisation.

However, we had some small wins. The head of IT and I worked together to change the activation email so it actually looked like an official email from the company providing extra guidance to the customers, and we managed to make small changes to the dead-end page customers were taken to. Probably the biggest achievement was getting the head of IT to see things from a user-experience point of view and to appreciate the impact of selecting a product purely from a technical perspective.

While you will come up against obstacles that are hard and sometimes impossible to shift, there will be many more times when having design embedded in an agile team will allow you to pivot quickly. We were working with a client to reimagine their 25-year-old legacy system, and the tech lead and I worked together to decide upon the best tech stack.

Two weeks into development, we found that many of the common components needed a lot of re-work to function correctly, which was taking up a lot of development time, and if it continued, it could impact our velocity and user experience. We decided it was best to pivot quickly and change the tech stack before we went any further. It was the right decision—the new components were quicker to implement, the team was much happier, our velocity increased, and the customers saw value earlier on.

As with any organisation you work for, you never know what you're going to be dealing with until you're there. Changing technology inside an organisation isn't easy, and many tech decisions might originally have been made from a tech and cost perspective, rather than a user-experience perspective. So, whether you're a designer coming out of university, going from agency life to consulting, or working for a company or a government department where you want to lead as a designer, it's important to understand that you may not be working with the latest and most innovative technology to solve problems. You may not have huge budgets to work with or a development team that understands the value of design. You may find yourself working for a company that has great, complex problems to solve but has made poor tech choices that impact the customer experience, requiring you to think of workarounds and solutions.

All of these scenarios require design leadership and offer challenges and opportunities to create something better. If you find yourself within a design team at a product company or consultancy, I can't emphasise enough the importance of ensuring design is embedded within development teams and a customer and user mindset is instilled across the organisation. Wherever you find yourself on your journey, if you spot an issue, don't see it as someone else's problem to solve. Leaders lead—so lead.

We don't all speak the same language

Just as developers have their own language, so do we designers. We can go to any design event or join a design team and we'll all understand each other. We use the same geeky design phrases and have similar pet peeves.

Being a design leader in the tech world is different. You don't need to be fluent in both languages, but you do have to be bilingual enough to get by. Communication is vital if we're going to succeed in embedding design, so if the people you're addressing don't speak your language, it's your job to help them understand design in a way that works for them.

Agile development teams are fast paced. As a designer, you're working on the upcoming stories and testing on users; meanwhile, in parallel, you're getting cards ready for development by working with the BAs. You've got to make sure the multiple developers who are all working on different cards understand the requirements and expectations from the get-go.

You need to answer any design questions that arise while they're working on the cards, check their progress, while also working through tech problems such as bugs or scenarios that haven't been considered. You'll also be testing the current build version on users and highlighting any issues, which will then be prioritised before possible solutions are designed and tested. These eventually become story cards and get built—and the evolution of the product continues.

On top of all this work on the process, you're also trying to ensure design is embedded across both the team and the organisation. You may also be doing this as the only designer on the team.

In a tech consultancy, at the same time as you're working with the client, you'll also be working to upskill your company on design. It's like having multiple jobs that all require 100% of your brain and time. This is why it's so important to have a collaborative and supportive team that work together—and for that, you've got to be communicating well.

There is a huge amount of juggling, so the smoother you can make the process, the better (see Figure 3.1). I'm still refining the 'perfect' solution, and with every new client or new team the goalposts change—but new ideas always come to light. On top of pairing designers with developers, I find that running regular 30-minute design sessions, where you bring the whole team up to speed on

> **"There is always a lot of juggling, so the smoother you can make the process, the better."**

Then

Designs previously created

Pairing with developers as they work on stories previously created

Ensure the team are thinking with a customer mindset

Getting feedback from customers as we build

Re-design in the moment if something doesn't work

Now

Designs that need to be ready

Finalising designs to be built next

Refine designs based on customer feedback

Ensure designs consider the customers, tech and business

Working with the BA, PO, Tech Lead, Security champion to ensure there is a clear understanding and finalise last details

Later

Solutions to create

What research do we need to do for the next phase of the project

Workshops and research to understand the next phase

Co-creating initial ideas and solutions with the team

Gathering customer insights and feedback

Testing ideas and solutions with the help of the team

Feedback research and insights to the team

Do we need to spike something in code

Future

Don't forget where you're going

Keeping the North Star in mind as designs are created

What's new that can help us create something better?

Figure 3.1 Phases of a designer in an agile team

design and usability testing, helps reduce repeating the same information—especially important if you're all working remotely.

One of the most common issues I find is the lack of understanding about what a designer does and the different types of designers. This is a slow, uphill battle with many clients, tech consultancies and development teams because they simply don't know that not every designer is a visual designer, nor is every designer a researcher or product strategist—they don't understand what our titles mean. Putting a pure researcher on a product development team will give you great insights into what your customers think and whether it's the right thing to build, but it's not going to give you the slick, polished UI.

Everyone wants to ensure that the product, team and client are successful, so any skills gaps on the team need to be highlighted as a risk to the success of the project. If you're on a team and see a skills gap or are shaping a team and know there are specific design skills that will be needed, be sure to call it out and explain why either a different designer or additional designers will be required. While many of us can work across a variety of design skills, the majority of designers have their own core strengths.

Creating strong teams and successfully transitioning people in and out of longstanding accounts requires deep knowledge of what makeup of skills is needed for the team to be successful—both now and when transitions happen. These decisions often fall on people who are not directly involved in the project or who may not fully understand all the specific skills required; those close to the account have to ensure that what's needed is well communicated through the appropriate channels. One of our responsibilities as DesignedUp leaders is to make sure decision-makers are armed with the knowledge they need to make the right choices.

It's also important that the client understands the risks associated with not having the person with the right skills on a team. If you leave others to have this conversation on your behalf, they may not portray the specific risks from a design perspective as well as you would yourself, so be part of these conversations. At the same time, you'll be helping the decision-makers understand design better, and they can also help you shape your design language into business language. Getting everyone together in this way helps prevent misunderstandings and ensures design has a voice at the decision table.

At the end of the day, as a design leader, it falls to you to make sure that (a) the client understands what design skills are required to deliver the project successfully, and (b) all aspects of the project you're working on are communicated effectively to the right people. And if that means putting a bit more effort into developing your cross-discipline language skills, then that's what you need to do.

Non-believers

Being a consultant is like a game of cards: you never know what hand you're going to get. You can help shape the team your consultancy will be providing to some extent, but you never know what the client or the team at their end will be like. At Thoughtworks, we have blended teams (if the client has the capabilities) of client staff or other consultants they use and our own Thoughtworks consultants.

This blended approach enables us to share our knowledge and set the client up for continuing success once we've finished the project, but it does mean you never know what kind of team you're going to end up with. As designers, we can deal with this ambiguity; we're used to problem solving. I've been very lucky in that I've been able to convert many team members into thinking with a customer mindset, and I've also been successful in overcoming difficult clients and bringing them along on the design journey. However, there will always be times when you just can't talk people around, and their 'non-believer' attitudes can damage projects.

I was once part of a small team that was charged with rescuing a large government project. The client had created a team with multiple individual contractors, all of whom had different views and no clear way of working, even after working together for months. The project manager had promised the world to stakeholders and delivered barely anything, the budget was haemorrhaging and there were team arguments every day. By day three of my colleague and my starting on the rescue mission, between the time I left the office and the time I got home, one of the contractors had been walked off the project. It was clear the team was in a bad place and needed a reset.

We ran a two-week inception to unpack the problem they were trying to solve, created an agreed way of working that everyone was behind and defined each of the roles. We also put together a full end-to-end user journey and created a story map. This had never been done with them before, but we needed the whole team to see the full extent of what they were actually trying to build and the problems that really needed solving. This enabled us to define a thin end-to-end slice that allowed us to both fully test a complete flow with users and also make sure everything was technically possible across the most complex features. It gave the team something that worked within their timeframe and could be built upon slice by slice.

A couple of weeks down the line, we seemed to be in a good place. The independent contractors appeared engaged, and we thought we could work with them as one happy team. However . . .

We quickly discovered that the QA on our team wasn't familiar with agile and had an old way of working, but she seemed keen to learn. The other issue I recognised pretty much right away was with one of the developers, who would often try to solve user problems without talking to me or anyone else on the team. Rather than being collaborative, he would go directly to the product owner, explain his idea, and the product owner would agree. I would see odd changes happening in the test environment and then find out the product owner hadn't understood what he was agreeing to, which started causing re-work. I knew the developer was just trying his best to solve a problem he'd discovered, so I tried working more closely with him to get him to understand the new way of working and explaining my rationale for design decisions.

It soon became apparent that both the QA and the developer thought they were designers. I'm all for the team's being involved in design and bringing their ideas to the table, but their argumentative nature and refusal to listen to the customer insights and well-proven design interactions was something I hadn't experienced before. Sometimes, when people will simply not agree with you, you start to question yourself: Have I made the right decision? Are they right, do they know more than I do? The imposter syndrome can come in waves in these situations.

It turned out the QA was just a small concern, and I had bigger fish to deal with. After mapping out the full user journey, we discovered there were elements that had not been considered that would affect the design currently being built. I worked with our business analyst and tech lead to develop a solution that would be easy to implement and would make more sense to the user, then ran the idea past the product owner, who agreed, but the 'problematic' developer fundamentally hated the idea. On a day I wasn't working, he and the QA went behind my back to convince the product owner not to go ahead with my solution and tried to sell him a different idea.

It was clear I needed to take back control and stamp my authority as the design lead on the project. So I sat down with the product owner and BA, and we sketched out every scenario and design option, including the one the developer had suggested (which wouldn't have worked). Once we'd walked through everything and agreed (again) on the original solution, I got the developer on a call to run through everything. He seemed okay and I thought the matter was resolved.

It was not. To put an end to the madness, I gathered the entire team together, went through the user scenarios and the problem we were trying to solve, and presented the three different solutions. These were now nice-looking prototypes, to make it easier for everyone to understand the different user flows.

This meeting was to get all of us aligned as a team, decide which gave the best user experience and investigate whether there were any other solutions we hadn't considered. The tech lead, who was very user-focused, mentioned that the solution the product owner liked was something he'd seen in other software, and it would work well for the problem we were trying to solve.

The developer still couldn't get his head around it, stormed out of the meeting and went home. This should have been a simple problem to solve, but his refusal to accept that he was wrong and his inability to be a team player had temporarily derailed the project and kept us all away from more important work.

When you're trying to deliver a project that's costing the client millions, you just can't have someone like that on the team—you've got to be able to work collaboratively and trust each other. The client later made the decision to get rid of both the QA and the developer—and not just because of the issues I encountered.

When we did usability testing just after the developer walked out, every user flew through the solution that he had been so against, without any issues. They loved it. It's sad that he didn't stay around to see the final outcome.

As a design leader, it's inevitable that you'll come up against non-believers every now and then. Rather than arguing, being submissive or backing down, get everyone on the team involved and go through the problem and scenarios. Many brains are better than one—and get feedback from users to validate the solution. Most of the time, you should be able to bring people around so that everyone is behind the solution. However, you've got to accept that sometimes you will simply have to get rid of people in order to ensure the whole team performs and the project gets delivered.

When your go-to ways don't work

With our innate problem-solving skills, we designers are well suited to working in an agile environment, especially for a consultancy, where things move fast and you need to be on your feet, always thinking and solving problems. However, when it comes to being a DesignedUp leader, you'll often find yourself fixing people issues or organisational problems, rather than traditional design-specific problems. And although you might know what you need to achieve for success, you'll sometimes need to try a new approach to getting there.

The majority of people we work with throughout our careers are open to trying new ways of problem solving and are happy to trust and follow our process, but there will always be points in your career where you meet some individuals or teams who are resistant. It could be someone in a workshop who refuses to participate, or a client who can't see there is an issue because they are blinded by past experiences and have tarnished you with the same brush.

It's easy to take this personally and feel that you're failing, so it's important to remember that with any approach, method or piece of advice, there will always be people who just don't get it. Sometimes it's the concept itself that they struggle with; sometimes it's the analogy or technique you're using that they just don't like; and sometimes it's the language. Your challenge is to identify what's not working and find an alternative that does. Successful problem solving in an agile working environment is a team effort that spans the whole organisation, so you've got to get people on board.

I was discussing this topic with Luciana Albuquerque Gissing, Creative Director, Experience Design at Deloitte Digital in LA. She found herself consulting with a large gambling company and running a workshop with the execs:

> They were very dry and not collaborative. I have learnt from that and now make sure I have a co-facilitator and ensure they understand that the workshop will be hands-on—it's not going to be a presentation . . . If you can see who is coming in advance, you can prepare and tailor the workshop content better and you can adapt.

I absolutely agree that one of the most important things is making sure your attendees have been properly briefed about what the session will be like. So, just as you do with your clients, set expectations early to avoid confusion.

You may also find yourself in a situation where users are not expressing their views because their boss is in the room—or they just agree with everything their boss says. This really doesn't help when you're trying to get to the root of a problem and gain different perspectives. You can try to alter things by changing direction, such as by breaking people into smaller groups to capture their thoughts and problems. They then share these back to the whole group, which helps show the variety of perspectives and gives everyone the opportunity to add their opinions.

Often, the client doesn't know how diverse you need a workshop group to be or what stakeholders are necessary and why, so have a planning meeting with the client a few weeks before, and tell them specifically who you would like there. If you happen to be running a workshop where you don't know who is attending or you have some last-minute people show up, ice-breakers and quick introductions are a great way to find out who is in the room or on the Zoom® call; this helps you plan who will be in each group or breakout room to ensure you have a balance of perspectives.

And here's a good tip: if you receive advance notifications of additional attendees that you weren't expecting—perhaps because your client has forwarded on your e-invite—a quick LinkedIn® stalk can reveal if a CEO has been added to your meeting 10 minutes before it's about to start. That can allow you to quickly prepare and formulate a more CEO-appropriate conversation—and, yes, I'm speaking from experience! Luckily that one went well.

While some workshops and meetings will be challenging and test your resourcefulness —and patience!—at the other end of the spectrum, you can have participants who are incredibly collaborative, and you have to change the workshop up on the fly.

I was leading a co-design session with a group of users where each team was going through a 6-up sketching exercise. It quickly became apparent that everyone was on the same page and all had the same ideas, so instead of continuing, I changed direction and facilitated all of them sketching out their combined solution on a large wall. Although these particular users worked in different teams within the organisation and had different requirements, they were thrilled to all be involved in shaping the new software they were going to be using.

A design leader knows when to change direction and isn't afraid to do so. In an agile environment, this is even more important, because you need to get the feedback from users quickly in order to validate an idea so that you can pivot if needed, refine and prioritise, to make sure you design and build the 'right thing'.

Lead by example

The research of Marcin Treder (Senior UX Design Manager, Google®/LinkedIn) revealed that lo-fi prototypes are not popular with clients—what they want are full, hi-res, pixel-perfect designs so they can see exactly what they're going to get for their money. Meanwhile, we know that a hi-fi design isn't always necessary, unless you're creating hi-fi prototypes to test the micro interactions, because that's how people use apps, like Instagram do. However, every design starts with an idea, a rough sketch. We need to lead by example and show them how our way of thinking and working can help them achieve the best outcomes.

We were building an MVP and needed a quick solution for a particular screen. It didn't need to be a slick design but had to look better than a bunch of numbers and text that had been pulled in from the database. We knew that we'd come back and make it slick once we'd tried and tested the solution, but it still needed to be functional and intuitive for the MVP users.

Before we started working with the client, designs were created by whoever owned the requested feature, such as the head of the customer engagement team, whom was neither a designer nor developer.

This caused a number of issues—the designs and functionality were often created based on examples they had seen in other products, which weren't compatible with the tech stack they were using and caused issues with the developers trying to get things to work as desired. The designs were also not tested with customers, and the feature ideas were driven from within the business rather than from the customer, resulting in features being built that had a very low uptake.

Our approach of continuous usability testing was a completely new concept and way of working for the organisation. Due to the history of features' being owned by people who were not close to the technology, it was important to ensure the organisation was taken along on the journey of both testing early and upskilling departments to improve their design maturity and approach to building the right thing in an incremental way.

To show the client a better way of working and create the quick solution we needed to improve the way the data was displayed, I paired with a developer, and we sketched out some options. Working together, we quickly moved from sketches to something that looked pretty good in code. I took photos of us working and presented our approach in the companywide showcase for our product.

Although this is a normal thing for designers to do, we need to remind ourselves that what's normal to us is not normal for everyone. Showing examples and talking openly about how we work and the outcomes we create helps organisations feel more comfortable in knowing they don't need hi-res, perfect solutions all the time. And once they can see how lo-fi prototypes and designer/developer pairings speed up delivery—which makes their budget go further and still produces an excellent solution—they soon become advocates.

Building relationships is also crucial to your success, as you will often be working with people who are new to their roles and out of their comfort zone, so they may want to take the 'safe' path for fear of messing up. I was working on a project that had appointed a product owner who, as head of one of the departments, was also one of the users. He was lovely and had a huge wealth of knowledge in his specialism, which was a tremendous help. However, it was his first time in the role and his first time creating a digital platform. He was keen to wait until the first release was ready before testing on our different cohorts, and he also wanted to make sure the new platform was somewhat complete before showing them. From conversations, I knew he was under the impression that his entire team used the same processes as he did to gather the information, enter the information and use the outdated software in the same way he did.

Anyone who has ever tested a prototype or observed people using digital products knows that everyone does things in a slightly different way—even if it's standard software, they will find workarounds or shortcuts. People learn and understand by observing and experiencing something for themselves, so I needed to take the product owner along on the journey and show him the value in testing as we went.

The trust I had built with him meant it was a quick and simple conversation. I explained the advantages of testing early and how getting feedback from our users would allow us to ensure we built the right thing and adhered to the product vision.

The first official round of testing the clickable prototypes demonstrated the value in usability testing by highlighting areas that worked and areas where we could make minor improvements, and the conversations with the users allowed us to uncover additional pains they were experiencing with the old system that had not been shared before during research.

It also showed that the users within the product owner's team all did things slightly differently. The initial round proved the value in testing early and allowed us to scale the efforts by developing continuous usability testing sessions, virtual co-design sessions and an online chat group giving us direct access to users at any time.

If I had my time again . . .

As designers and leaders, we're always looking around us for influence—looking at the future and new technology trends to help solve problems and looking at other industries for those 'Aha!' moments. We're always searching for answers, trying to improve our skills and how we work, develop better solutions, disrupt what we have and pivot.

But if design leaders could have their time again, what advice would they give their younger selves? As design leaders, how can we work to ensure those we're

> **We need to remind ourselves that what is normal to us is not normal for everyone.**

mentoring don't make the same mistakes we did? Jennifer Martin, Associate Partner, Asia Pacific Experience Design Leader at EY, had this to say:

> If I had to do it over, I'd get a variety of experience early on in my career. There are many benefits of working for massive international consultancies, but I always wonder what it would have been like to work in agencies, in-house, start-ups, etc. before selecting a specialty.

Be comfortable with change

The consultant life is a challenge. Every time you start a new project, it's like starting a new job—new place, new people, new rules of engagement—which can be taxing and tiring. You need to be comfortable with change because it's part of the job. To manage this, make sure you take enough time or do what works best for you to 'reset your head' before moving from one project to another.

You'll need to learn to be comfortable being uncomfortable.

Maria Gomez, Director of Engineering, BCG Digital Ventures

Embrace ambiguity

You never know what you're going to face when you start a new project. What a client tells you during pre-project meetings and anything disclosed during an RFP process are never the full story. You may also be helping with some of their biggest challenges, where they don't have all the answers, and you're entering the domain with little information. You need to be okay with ambiguity and trust the process of discovering what the problem is, then finding a solution together. The solution may or may not work, and you need to be okay with that as well—it's a journey of discovery.

As a consultant you'll need to be comfortable sitting in the unknown yourself and helping others sit there as well. Many clients are not accustomed to collaborative sessions, where you start peeling back the layers and diverging to understand the problem—some expect you to go straight in with the answers and just get working. You need to help them trust the journey and explain WHY you're doing what you're doing—that will help them feel more comfortable. Jennifer added:

> You need to be comfortable working with incomplete information. More important, you need to lead others who are uncomfortable and get them to trust the process.

Take the big picture view

Many consultants, especially lateral hires and those coming from an agency, haven't always had the opportunity to see the bigger picture and the overall strategy of where their clients are heading or how and where their piece of work fits as part of the whole.

Those who have already run and managed their own smaller agencies, where they've had the opportunity to understand their clients' businesses, have a better grasp on this. However, the types of clients that large consultancies work with are generally large organisations with multiple locations. As a DesignedUp leader, your mission is to understand how the structure works and what motivates the decision-makers. Sofia Woods, Product Design Director at Xero, had this to say:

> Being a design consultant means the smallest amount of my work is dedicated to 'actual visual design'. Design is much, much bigger than the UI, and to be a valuable design consultant, you need to build an understanding of the work you're doing in the context of both the customers *and* the business. What's the vision and the strategy? Much of my time is understanding these elements and then helping my team make the connections between these and the work we're doing.

Ask deeper questions

As well as understanding the bigger picture, you need to ask the client broader questions to understand the real state of the situation or company position—immerse yourself in what matters to the business. The questions you ask will also depend on who you're speaking to—is it a stakeholder for your particular project or a team of execs?

You could ask questions like: 'What is your biggest problem?' 'What about this worries you the most?' 'Do you agree it's a big problem, as we do?' 'What is your objective—is it growth, retaining customers, reducing costs?' If the stakeholder is in charge of the project you're about to work on, you could ask: 'What are we trying to do for the customer? Are we helping them do something faster [better, more effectively . . .]?' Asking simple questions like these will open up the conversation and show the client you really want to understand the situation, which also helps build trust. This information gathering will later help you define the right metrics (as we'll discuss in Chapter 4). A technical leader at one of the Top 4 consultancies advises:

> Career wise, get into consulting early. In an agency you can hit a ceiling before too long. If you're at the top of your discipline and you're not running the business, you've hit the ceiling. At a consultancy there is a whole different career ladder. Join a consultancy that has a strong agency pedigree, that's the area where you can learn the most.

Get comfortable with multiple languages

To communicate effectively, we need to be able to explain our processes and justify our decisions to those who don't have a design background or think in the same way that we do. This can be hard in the agile consulting world, when you're constantly moving to different teams and having to learn again how best to communicate with the new people. You might need to up your knowledge on different areas or spend some time understanding different personality types. Here are some tips:

- Learning more about back-end and data structures can help you conceptualise designs and communicate with developers and quality analysts.
- Having front-end knowledge will help you speak to developers and enable you to properly size the effort of what you're asking.
- Acquiring more business language will enable you to explain to execs the advantage of spending time on UI design, testing or creating a styleguide. You can explain the risks it reduces and the advantage this gives the business in a more empathetic way, giving you a greater chance of success.
- Being able to communicate effectively with the head of delivery means you can properly explain the risk of not spending extra time to test a concept.

One design consultant I interviewed share this:

> You'll develop opinions on things you didn't think you needed to have an opinion on. The question isn't whether designers should code, but how can designers work with technologists? You've navigated these spaces before, and you'll have to dig to remember the ways you explored in different contexts—working with freelancers, IT departments, small orgs—all of it.

Be aware of how your audience thinks

Some find it hard to get their head around the process we undertake when we're solving a problem. We have to go broad to understand the full problem and look at potential solutions, and we're always working to achieve the vision of the product. We use this process continuously—it could be at the beginning of an innovation project or at various stages on a delivery project—where we're regularly conducting usability testing to gain feedback and have to do a mini-version of divergent and convergent thinking, delving deeper into the problem and looking at different options to solve it.

The process commonly known as the 'Double Diamond' is undertaken by designers before it had a name and where the problem is regarded as just as important as the solution. We explore the problem (divergent thinking), then narrow it down and define the problem (convergent thinking). We then divert again and explore solutions until we converge to the solution. This then leads into prototyping, usability testing, iterating and building (Design Thinking). It's not a linear, step-by-step process, and we will repeat it any number of times, incorporating the new information we discover about the problem from usability testing and tech constraints as we go.

This is all a natural process for us; however, some people find it hard to grasp and think we are overthinking or 'gold plating' the solution unnecessarily. Sometimes, people see a great solution in what we're presenting and expect they're going to get the gold version immediately, then are disappointed when the design is broken down into small pieces and delivered over time with regular releases. And sometimes, no matter how much you involve developers in the process, some will agree that a particular desired outcome you've landed on will be easy to achieve, then when it comes down to implementation, different developers will disagree.

While using the Double Diamond and Design Thinking diagrams can be useful visual indicators, the danger is that it can result in individuals or organisations getting the impression that this is a 'one-time-only' process. And if you don't explain it clearly, they could misunderstand how much time and work there is still to go.

We know that the creation of any digital product, service or customer experience is not a linear process, and the process length can change, depending on the problem. So, always be aware of who your audience is, and make sure they understand this.

Say 'No' without saying 'No'

I'm notoriously bad for saying 'Yes' and overcommitting myself, so it's comforting to know that many other design leaders suffer the same fate. I think it's a design thing —we want to solve all the problems. So, before you commit to something (I'm trying to do this myself), think about whether it aligns with where you're heading and if it's going to help you get there, even indirectly.

Decide what you're able or want to do, then turn down the other requests. Avoid saying 'No, I don't want to do that', or 'No, it's not my thing', as 'No' is a pretty harsh, negative word, and if you use it too often, people may stop asking you anything at all—which can result in your missing out on opportunities you actually want!

When turning something down, Kevin Yeung takes this approach:

> I'd ask clarifying questions and urge them to talk through their problem so I can understand what they want to achieve. Then if it's not my area of expertise, I can think about the best person to recommend; I can say, 'I think this person could really help', or 'Actually, I think the client needs this rather than what you're proposing'.

These are diplomatic ways of letting someone down. Nobody wants to work with difficult people, so it's important to understand that while your focus might be on one thing, someone else's agenda and priorities can be completely different.

Designers need to be around designers

Some consultancies place designers on their own on projects, which can work with the right designer who has tenure, a breadth of design skills, leadership and the right team around them. These consultants tend to bounce ideas off their teammates to gather different perspectives; however, there is nothing like thinking a problem through with other designers, especially ones who have complementary skills. While many designers are 'T-shaped', you can't be a master of everything. So, to prevent you from becoming isolated and feeling like you're not progressing—or if you just need some help in an area that's not your specialism—lean on your community within the consultancy.

For example, I don't have a deep knowledge of research; I can conduct research but not to the same depth as an actual design researcher. Thankfully, we have very good researchers within our design community at Thoughtworks who I chat to and discuss ideas and best approaches with.

So don't underestimate the importance of getting involved in the design community within the consultancy—maybe your consultancy has several communities that interest you. The friends you make there will give you comfort, make work fun and share their collective wisdom with you. It's also a 'safe' place to share early ideas, and you can all relate to annoying problems and help each other get through the tough days.

> ## You'll be happiest with a design pair.
> ## Try to get one on your project.
> Design consultant

Never underestimate your influence

You are where you are because of your knowledge and skills, and clients want to learn from you, just as you need to learn from them to help solve their problems. You can have a profound amount of influence, so always speak up, share your opinions and make sure design has a voice, says one design consultant:

> You'll spend a lot of time introducing processes to your team that you know are fundamental to design and marketing. Just because everyone is so smart and talented doesn't mean you don't have something to teach them.

Don't pretend to be a unicorn

The majority of people don't know what a designer does, or they have preconceived ideas and notions. 'You just produce this magic, it's impressive', was a comment I received from a team member after presenting at a showcase. Whether there is one designer or many on your team, always set the expectations early as to what your specific design skills are, and don't be ashamed that you're not great at everything—you're not supposed to be! A design consultant I interviewed advised:

> Focus on what you do and what you bring—empathy, facilitation, collaboration, synthesis—whatever it may be; find moments to bring that into your team, project, etc.

Helping younger consultants navigate our world

While lateral hires or the more senior designers who've joined the consultancy world through acquisition have adjustments to make and need to understand how to navigate and carve a career in the new landscape, because of their tenure they've been around long enough to understand how organisations operate, and they tend to have a high level of confidence. However, leaders who have been in the consulting industry for a while are noticing certain common traits with younger designers joining this world. Some of these traits are huge positives, but with others they'll have to reset their expectations. As design leaders, we need to help them navigate these issues—even if we've never faced them ourselves:

Pay. Some leaders have experienced younger designers making comments like, 'I'd earn more at Google'. They've left university with the impression they are an unstoppable first-class designer and don't fully understand that they lack a lot of the skills required if you want to be paid the big bucks. They don't understand what it actually costs to run a business and that a consultancy needs to manage project margins and ensure their rates make them competitive but still profitable.

Not taking advice. Some leaders have experienced younger consultants not acting on feedback they've been given. Rather than talking through the why or making changes to their design based on the feedback, the younger designer responds with: 'Ummm, I think I'll just leave it as it is'. If the designer is that sure and passionate about their solution, they should be able to explain their rationale but then also appreciate the value in listening to and learning from the views of others. For younger designers reading this, remember to keep an open mind—the designer is not always right, and almost never first time! As design leaders, we will need to coach them to take a more human-centred approach—certainly get them to test their idea and see whether there's common feedback.

Hierarchy. 'It seems very hierarchical', and, 'You seem to know a lot', are comments that design leaders in consultancies have heard from more junior colleagues. So we need to work on getting these younger consultants to understand that not every company is flat or structured like a start-up, and there should be a level of respect for those who've proven themselves and gained knowledge and expertise over time. The arrogance around thinking they know everything isn't just related to design—I've seen the same attitude in some developers and can only assume it's coming from particular universities, where students leave feeling they are somehow part of an elite. Again, it's our job to help them navigate this and shape them into more humble humans.

Knocking it out of the park. Although some universities seem to be breeding elitists who struggle to adapt in the consulting world, others are creating great consultants who can clearly articulate the thinking and reasoning behind their design. They are often good at navigating the latest design software, preparing presentation decks and documents, and they learn quickly. While some have the consulting part nailed, they do often struggle with refining their deliverables—but this is something design leaders can easily help them with. We must also make sure we encourage these design leaders of the future to have the confidence to try lots of new things that will expand their skills.

The truth no one tells you

So, when it comes down to it, what's it really like to be a design leader? Is it as glorious as the articles you've read or the conference speakers you've listened to? Will you really always be working with cool tech, solving the world's biggest problems, have a team of designers to work with, be able to drive change and work with cutting-edge organisations that champion design and love it as much as you do? Um, I'm afraid not.

However, even if you won't always be on the 'coolest' projects, the ones you're on will often consist of complex problems that require challenging technological solutions while still delivering a great experience. And the stakeholders and the organisations they work for may need their hands held as you take them on the journey to solving the problem.

Even though some of the biggest names in Silicon Valley have built exceptional design capabilities themselves, they still work with some of the largest consultancies. You may get to work with them; however, you probably won't be working on their innovation projects. More likely you will be working in areas that are very complex, even for them, or in an area where they just don't have specific expertise and don't intend on growing any expertise in that area—a particular tech stack, for example.

Not all the large organisations or government departments are ready to adopt VR, AR or XR or have a need for designing engaging voice-first experiences. They either want to see how users adopt the technology first, have an innovation department focusing on new emerging technologies, or simply have bigger digital transformation problems to solve. And many large organisations that have been around for years find it hard to pivot and become digital and customer focused. We saw how many large brands—even those that already had seemingly good online experiences—struggled with their online services when demand surged overnight with the onset of COVID and lockdown.

A technical leader at one of the Top 4 consultancies remarked in an interview:

> I always say to the juniors, if what they were trying to do wasn't difficult, they wouldn't need the likes of us to come in. You won't always get to work on the latest tech, but you get to work on the things people will actually pay for, and if we as leaders do our jobs, then it's usually solving pretty interesting problems.

So, while you won't necessarily be working on the latest innovations all the time, you will be working on interesting and complex problems. Sometimes you'll be solving everyday issues faced by the general public, another time you could be helping resolve a safety problem for people on an oil rig that's miles out at sea. You might be improving the customer experience across a global fleet of cruise lines, or you might need to understand how a group of scientists do their work so you can create a system that will save them time and accurately capture all their vital data, ensuring the correct policies are put in place to ensure the flora and fauna we know today stays around for generations to come.

While you won't necessarily be working on projects that will hit the headlines as cutting-edge advancements, some of the projects will most definitely hit the headlines if they fail and waste millions in taxpayers' money or become the biggest technology failure of the year! Some consultancies have social justice projects that people can get involved in when they're not on client projects—such as solving a problem for medical staff working with patients effected by a deadly disease or a pandemic. They might have artist-in-residence projects, where technologists and artists work together; or you might get to spend 20% of your time working on a personal project that is relevant to the industry.

Depending on the consultancy or tech company, you may find yourself the only designer on a team or project, as I've mentioned a few times. Then, it will be your sole responsibility to take every client on the design journey to understand what design really is and the value it adds. You will need to build relationships constantly, and when there is a restructure, which happens often in these organisations, you may feel like you're always building new relationships and having to find new advocates for design.

I can guarantee it will sometimes feel like 'Groundhog Day', but you need to keep the end goal in mind. With every person you manage to take along on the design journey, whether they stay at the organisation or get replaced, that's one extra person who understands the value of design.

Although not everyone in your consultancy will have worked with a designer before, you're all united in your common objective: to do a great job, solve the customer's problem and work as a team. You will therefore find everyone is keen to learn more about design and help you on your mission, although this still requires you to step up and be the positive force—the one who's passionate about design.

You need to instil in them a desire to follow you, learn about design and help you, which will never happen if you stay quiet or continually complain about the team or client 'not getting it'. All teamwork is two-way, so make sure you give back and listen to other people's ideas—remember, just because you're the designer doesn't mean you have all the answers. A diverse group of minds results in better questions and better solutions.

After asking developers what 'new' thing they had learnt from working with a designer, some of the responses I got demonstrate the importance of educating everyone we come into contact with:

> 'The new thing I learnt from working with a designer was understanding more about how delivery and design relate and how they impact each other'.
> 'I can now see that a designer is not a passive member on the team—they are there to influence many decisions'.

You will build friendships within your consultancy that make it feel like a family, and you will also build these bonds with clients and their teams, giving you multiple families and connections in different sectors. And many consultancies try extra hard to ensure their consultants feel supported. They know you're working with clients most of the time, either on site or remotely, and your team might feel disenfranchised from the rest of the consultancy; therefore, they put a lot of focus on making sure you feel united and supported.

On the social side, there are regular office or team lunches, where all the consultants get together in a home office; many teams moved this to lunches or drinks over Zoom during COVID. Some consultancies send 'care packages' out to you while you're onsite or at home, and many run regular social events, which are suggested and voted for by the consultants.

If you land at the right consultancy, they will also care about your career and give great guidance, direction and a coach, no matter what your level. They will allow you to pursue your passion and turn that into something that might fill a gap for clients or that they can see will become the next shift in the future.

I guarantee that sometimes it will feel like 'Groundhog Day'.

You will need a valid reason to pursue what you want, and there's got to be something in it for them—at the end of the day, they are a business—so make sure you do your research and can support your proposed career path with relevant evidence of how it will benefit the consultancy and their clients. It takes a lot of effort to find people who are great at their craft and make excellent consultants—if they've hired you, they're not going to want to lose you—so don't be afraid to speak up for what you want.

Consultancy life can take its toll, and sometimes you'll feel like you're constantly swimming against the tide. You'll be pulled between your passion for great design and technology challenges, business issues and budgets. You'll constantly be using your consulting skills to advocate for design—within both the client organisation and the consultancy—and will need to carefully balance client politics . . . all while meeting deadlines in a fast-changing environment.

Sometimes you'll just want breathing space—time to step back and think about the problem at hand to enable you to develop solutions, question things and simply focus on the design. I find I think better when I'm moving and away from my team and client—when it's just the spin bike and I or when I'm out for a run. Having 'thinking space' is important and often something you don't get when you're onsite, in an office that's not yours, or on Zoom calls and workshops for most of the day. So, make sure you create space for yourself, and remember that stepping out of one environment and into another can often make all the difference.

So, in summary . . .

The consulting world will bring new challenges and open your eyes to new opportunities, new problems and new skills, but it's hugely important that you bring your past experiences with you. The skills and qualities you learnt in the design world will help differentiate you, both inside your consultancy and with clients.

You need to think bigger as a consultant. Where does the problem you're working on start and finish, how does it fit within the wider organisation? Keep looking outwards for opportunities to increase your knowledge and grow your perception of design.

When your usual methods and approaches don't work, be comfortable and confident enough to pivot; always lead by example and find your advocates. The work may not always be glamorous or set the world on fire, but know that you will be helping organisations solve some of their most complex problems—the ones that keep executives awake at night.

Always advocate for more designers on a team; there are specialists for a reason, and having complementary skills promotes growth and produces better outcomes. And while you're reaching for the stars, don't forget to reach down and help younger design consultants. Your skills, knowledge and experience are what will help them navigate this world and build their own distinct career path.

―――――――――――

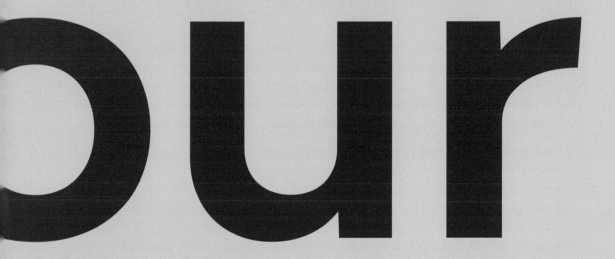

proving the power and value of design

Designers know the far-reaching value of design and that many products, experiences and systems—from the everyday to the exceptional—would not be what they are without it. To most people, design is ambiguous and messy, so as problem solvers, it's on us to help them understand the value of design and how best to use it. In this chapter you will learn how to get buy-in, how to measure the value of design that resonates with the business, and how to demonstrate the cost of not having designers involved.

a s designers, we all have this relentless passion for solving problems and designing beautiful, usable products. We want organisations to understand what we actually do and put design at the centre of their operation, not silo it away from the technology.

There is nothing more satisfying than watching someone use what you've designed and seeing how it's solved their problem, or seeing the smile on their face when what used to be hard to use is now easy and intuitive. As a visual designer, I love it when a user or a client gets excited by a new design. What was once confusing to navigate and increased the user's visual stress is now a great experience—more accurate, better functioning and a pleasure to look at and use every day.

However, tech consultancies are not always designing at the bleeding edge of innovation, and many are working with antiquated organisations that have never worked agile, let alone taken a design-centred approach. They're also often dealing with clients who want to re-imagine the customer experience but are held back by legacy systems and inefficient ways of working. It'll be your job to help change that.

We're all aiming for a great end result; however, getting there as a consultant in the tech world is not always smooth sailing. Many clients are hesitant to let you speak to their customers for fear they will be found out for having old technology, or the customers themselves will be reluctant to change the trusted product that they have come to rely on. It's not always glamorous work for designers, but it is incredibly valuable work that can completely change the way an organisation operates, so that they serve their customers better and their employees can perform everyday tasks more easily and efficiently. Being in a consultancy means you get to work with a variety of businesses, and the problems and solutions are always different. You've just got to be prepared to take the distinctly unsexy along with the super-cool.

And it's really satisfying to take clients and their employees along on the journey: helping them shift their mindset from thinking design is just making something look pretty to really understanding and experiencing the value of embedding designers within delivery teams, and how this ensures customer opportunities are discovered and the right problem is solved, and how approaching their problems from a design and tech perspective prevents their wasting millions of dollars building the wrong thing—now that's a worthwhile job.

Naturally, with each client you will be faced with different challenges. While interviewing 50 experience designers across consultancies, freelancers and in-house to understand the real-life UX design process, Marcin Treder (founder of UxPin® and Senior UX Design Manager at Google®) uncovered several challenges that were trending among the designers:

- Spreading an understanding of the design process. How to engage the whole team in the process.
- Communication within the team. How to communicate with a team throughout the process and use different perspectives of teammates to evaluate design deliverables.
- Demonstrating the process to get buy-in. How to present the design process to stakeholders and developers to actually get buy-in, both formally and psychologically.
- Testing lo-fi prototypes is not popular with clients.
- Tight budgets are forcing UX designers to tailor their processes and skip costly research.
- Mature organisations are afraid of 'guerrilla research' that is spontaneous, efficient and cheap.

Every project I've been involved with has required finding ways to overcome the above challenges and more. I've had to develop different ways to solve these issues and sometimes pivot when things haven't quite gone to plan.

Getting buy-in

Let's be honest—it's often frustrating being a designer. We understand the value that design can bring to the success of a project—we live and breathe it every day—and some clients get it, they really do. But then there's the majority that think they get it or say they understand and value it, but they really don't.

So the initial meetings seem positive: you discuss design and its value, and everyone is in agreement. Then it comes down to negotiating costs, and suddenly the value of design is questioned. There's still a perception by some that having more developers will get them where they need to go faster. This mindset means design often gets cut to a minimum or is even seen as a 'tick box' exercise so they can say they are being customer focused or using design thinking, without fully understanding what it means.

Too many organisations still view design as creating a pretty prototype without understanding the breadth of the field of design and all the areas where design can have a positive impact by constituting a great customer experience. They refer to great experiences that other brands have launched and want the same without understanding that those experiences might not be right for their customers or may not work with their systems. This lack of understanding and appreciation of the skill and effort that goes into researching, designing and creating the right exceptional experience is a constant problem.

Sometimes those working in the product delivery teams understand the value that design brings, but often the execs or middle management don't—they have different priorities. This means we're regularly having to share our knowledge and communicate our value in language they understand.

To add to that, many organisations that are undergoing digital transformation know they need to adapt and change in order to keep up, but their budgets are not infinite, and often they focus on the tech rather than design, simply because they don't know how design can help. They often don't understand the complexities and effort involved in creating the experiences they are so accustomed to using with brands like Amazon®, Google and leading digital product companies. And why should they? It's not on them to understand all the nuances of design; it's on us to help them understand, so it's essential we build trust, create impact and demonstrate value to our clients from day one. We have to show them by 'doing' and make sure we're visible. Your job is to lead the entire team and stakeholders to think with a customer mindset.

I find a great way to get people on board is to involve them in customer workshops and sketching sessions so they experience the design process first-hand. This is where having designers embedded works really well. The beauty of being the minority on a delivery team means you can always play the 'I need your help' card to gather user research and feedback. I tend to set the expectation early on that everyone on the team is responsible for the experience and that I require everyone to take part in at least one usability testing or research session. You need to get to know your team—some will be a little shy to volunteer, and everyone will need to be approached differently. That said, the majority of people are willing to help, even if it's just taking notes. Developers want to create software that customers love, just as designers do, and I find people from other departments are often keen to find out more about their customers.

Finding ways to effectively communicate with diverse teams and customers to get their buy-in requires empathy and being prepared to try different things until you find something that works. I've been in situations where quieter members on my team didn't feel comfortable conducting customer interviews, but I needed them to start seeing the product from a user's perspective, rather than through the same lens they'd had developing the old product that we were replacing. I spoke to them individually, emphasised why it was important for them to be involved and asked if they would be comfortable to simply sit in and observe the interview, to which they all agreed. Once they'd actually viewed the product we were creating from a different perspective, they got excited about solving the customer's problem and started thinking with a different mindset—it was really great to see.

Involving other teams in user research and usability testing is a great way to spread the love of design and build empathy for the customer across the organisation. I usually find the customer engagement and marketing teams are the easiest to build relationships with and recruit as advocates. Customer engagement teams or call centres are often the forgotten source of customer information, and you'll be amazed at what they know—by fixing customer issues, you'll be making their lives easier, so it's fairly straightforward to get them on your side. If they're getting fewer calls about resetting a forgotten password because the product didn't have a way for the customer to self-serve, they can focus on more important calls, which saves the organisation time and money. The customer wins, the business wins and the staff win.

Get everyone thinking like a customer

It's important that you set the right expectation at the start of a project and continuously plant the seed with your team about usability testing and the importance of thinking from a user's point of view. This is a critical element of the design process.

One of the projects I was involved in required us to take three legacy systems used by scientists and create one new system that all the teams could use. The way the scientists conducted their research was not in a lab but out in the field—among the rainforests, in the Outback, near water bodies, etc. It was highly interesting and diverse.

One of the first things we established was that every person already on the team and every new person joining the team, no matter what their role, would spend some time with one of the scientists out in the field (in this case, the closest woodland). They would walk through one of their methods, from how they collect the data to what they do to put it into the software once they get back into the office.

This gave the entire team a real context for the project right from the start—the scientists' processes, what the data means and why it's important, empathy for the user—and achieved a far greater impact than reading a persona on a wall ever could.

I presented this way of working at the initial showcase with stakeholders. The programme manager was a real advocate for being human centred and was excited to see we were instilling this mindset.

Showcasing the design process

Getting team members and others within the organisation involved in usability testing is one tool you can use to help them more clearly understand the design process, its value and their end customers. Another that I highly recommend is showcases.

All agile delivery teams have regular showcases of the projects they're working on. These are held at the end of each iteration (every two weeks), and depending on the size of the organisation, we usually have an open invitation to whoever wants to attend. During the showcase, we walk the audience through what we did during the iteration, what we learned from customers, what we have built and designed, what our next steps are, etc. We cover high-level information across business, technology and design.

This is the platform for you to wear your 'sales design hat' and really sell the value that design is creating for the organisation and the product you're building. I take the audience through what we've been doing, why we're doing it, the problems it solves for the user and, most importantly, what this means for the business—reduced calls to the call centre, faster data entry for their staff, etc. I cover everything—from the research phase through to showing lo-fi prototypes and later high-fi designs. I emphasise what design is and what it isn't, to drive home the point that design isn't just pretty pictures . . . although they do always seem to like my pretty pictures!

I usually get asked a lot of questions at the end, with people wanting to know more about design and the insights we've gathered. Many of the business people we present to are really keen to learn and get involved.

> ## I've not seen usability testing presented that way before. It's really powerful, clear and adds great value.
>
> Sarah Taraporewalla, Director of Enterprise Modernisation, Platforms and Cloud, Thoughtworks

It's significant that they don't walk away talking about the technology; they leave talking about the design, how it looks, how it functions, the problems it solves for their clients or users, the great comments from customers captured during usability testing that they can go on to use in marketing campaigns. People never leave talking about how great the tech stack is (sorry, engineers!); they only want to talk about the experience. The same goes for visual design—it's the thing people talk about and remember. Thanks to the superfast way the human brain operates, you have just 50 milliseconds before users have made their first judgements on your digital product,[*] so the immediate visual 'hit' is critical.

While showcases work brilliantly in terms of selling to the wider stakeholders, you still need team buy-in, which requires a more in-depth approach. Although we have daily stand-ups, it's hard in that short time to talk about design on a deeper level, and I'm often working with multiple developer pairs on different components at any one time, as well as talking to stakeholders and users. So to ensure the whole team understands where I am with design, get their buy-in and keep them user centred, I also run fortnightly 30-minute design sessions to bring them up to speed on everything and make sure everyone is on the same page. Figures 4.1a through 4.1d are examples of what I present in showcases.

---

[*] As evidenced in research by Gitte Lindgaard, Gary Fernandes, Cathy Dudek and J. Brown https://www.tandfonline.com/doi/abs/10.1080/01449290500330448

What did customers think about calling the group of collectors 'Site Visit Team'?

80%

Prefer the term 'Collectors' or 'Site Collectors'.

Figure 4.1a   Site Visit Team vote

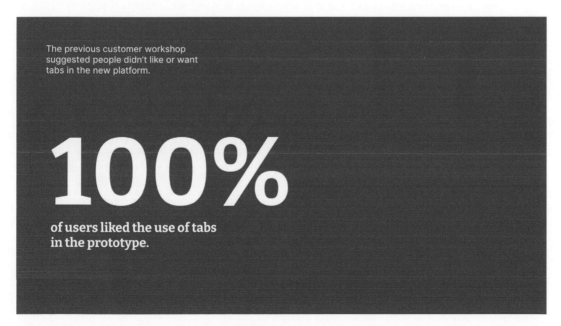

The previous customer workshop suggested people didn't like or want tabs in the new platform.

100%

of users liked the use of tabs in the prototype.

Figure 4.1b   100% vote for 'Tabs in the Prototype'!

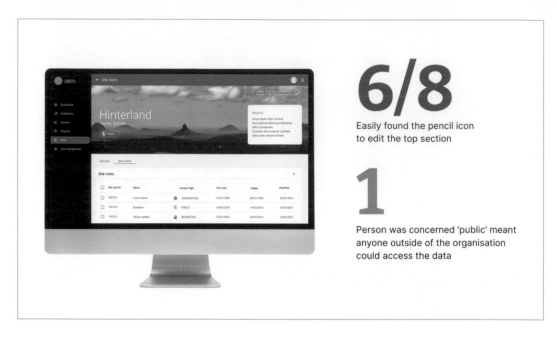

Figure 4.1c   Pencil icon vote, slight confusion over 'public'

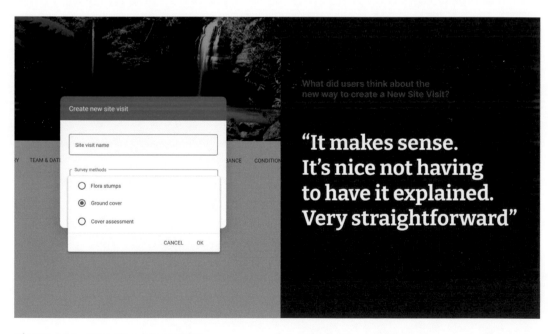

Figure 4.1d   New site visit reaction

The client has an idea you know is stupid

As designers, we are exposed to lots of different problems—it's the beauty of what we do. Whether you're in an agency or a consultancy, there will always be a time when the client has an idea that you know a user will hate or that just won't work. As DesignedUp leaders, we need to introduce clients to design reasoning to help them understand why.

I was running a discovery session with a group of C-level execs, and during one of the ideation sessions, an exec from the business side of the organisation had an idea: he wanted to incorporate a way for users to easily share their results on social media through the platform. He assumed that, as they were a young demographic and regularly shared their lives on social media, they would love the idea. However, when I added the idea to the mix and tested it during customer research sessions, every customer said how much they hated it! 'Hell no! That's kinda embarrassing!'

Although the younger generation do typically share a lot on social media, there are certain things in their lives that they want to keep private. I presented the findings to the organisation, and while they were surprised, they respected the research and we didn't build the feature, which saved them time and money and demonstrated just a tiny part of the value of the design process. Luckily, the person who came up with the idea just shrugged it off and didn't fight the evidence.

As I mentioned earlier, when presenting solutions to problems, you should use facts and data and have empathy for the person you're presenting to. It's exactly the same with ideas and solutions you don't think will work—present them with the research and data and don't directly disagree, as it can alienate you from the very client you're trying to help. When I discussed this topic with Evan Bottcher (Head of Architecture at MYOB), he had a really nice way to explain what your mindset should be: 'Disagree and Commit':

> Don't directly disagree—it's better to be there and to help than not be there. 'Disagree and commit' was a saying I learnt while working with one of the Big 4 banks. Don't undermine their decisions; collect the data as the direction is played out, limit the damage and give them the opportunity to pivot. Help them save face, as their career is invested. Join forces and share ideas, but bear in mind that your argument might not be enough to get it across the line, so get a qualitative view—data, money, risk and win; someone else is often then accountable. I can sleep well at night if I've given them the data and they've decided not to do it.

There will also be times when team members, peers or the client wants to try something, and either you know from experience it won't work or you're just not 100% convinced, but what they're proposing isn't going to be a huge disaster if it goes wrong. In that case, letting them run with it can be the best route forward—they'll either learn from the experience or maybe prove you wrong. People learn by doing, so you've got to allow them the space to try.

Budgets and being afraid of the unfamiliar

Every client faces budget issues—money just doesn't grow on trees, unfortunately! It's costly to build tech, and you can no longer build and forget. We have to continuously build, adapt to market conditions, allow for scale and keep up with the latest software releases, and just to add to the mix, customer demands are changing faster than ever. We're a demanding bunch of humans! As customers ourselves, we always expect the same experience from both large and small organisations, and if something doesn't work well, we'll happily swap to another product.

All this means brand loyalty is much harder to secure in today's world. Because customers make such quick first judgements on new digital products, software as a service (SaaS) companies that offer free trial runs have to convince customers very quickly that their product adds value and solves their problems. If they can't, the customer will take their business to a competitor, and you certainly don't want to let all the effort and money spent on acquiring these new customers go to waste. So, as design leaders, we need to deeply understand their business problems and find solutions that both work within the client's parameters and give customers a great experience.

Marcin Treder says that many mature organisations are afraid of guerrilla research. I'd go further and say that that applies to most businesses.

Many of the organisations I work with, both large and small, have never undertaken customer interviews, especially within the digital or IT departments, some of which have never had a designer embedded in a delivery team. Many have been nurturing the same clients for years, and letting a consultant they hardly know openly go and speak to them can be daunting. Either they're worried customers will panic when they find out the software they've been using for years is suddenly going to be replaced, or they've had bad experiences trying to get ideas from customers before. Some have over-promised and under-delivered in the past, resulting in fraught customer relationships.

Although it's understandable they feel as they do, as DesignedUp leaders, we need to help clients overcome their concerns. I achieve that by building relationships and trust with those who can give me access to the customers, explaining what I'm trying to do and the advantages it will give the organisation and the products they're building. I then invite them to join me on customer interview sessions and explain that we can try it first on the customers they feel most comfortable with.

A few years ago, I worked with a client who had these concerns. Once he had been to a few sessions with us, he quickly became comfortable with the process and even gave me the customers' phone numbers so I could organise interviews directly, rather than going through him. We ended up building great relationships with the customers, and the client was happy to follow our recommendations based on what we'd learnt, which really added value to the end product.

Fast-paced delivery teams with tight budgets and delivery deadlines don't always have the time or money for extensive research, even if they understand the value, but that's not an excuse for organisations not to do it—it just means we need to find something that works for them.

Using cohorts and the power of five is nothing new to designers, but it's something many clients aren't familiar with. I explain to them the advantages of identifying cohorts and how we can narrow research and testing by using just five people from each cohort. If there are a large number of cohorts, we can work together to prioritise them and then focus our research and testing efforts around the highest-priority groups. At this point, I usually find that clients swing in the opposite direction and go from not wanting any customer interviews to wanting to interview thousands!

Unfortunately, time and budgets are often strongly against us. In my experience, showing them some research on how patterns emerge after testing with five is usually enough to convince them—particularly if you use articles from established names, such as Nielsen Norman Group (a leader in the user experience field: nngroup.com). When the research with their own customers is complete and you can show how the patterns start to repeat, you tend to gain their full trust.

Once you've built a rapport with the customers, having a small pool that you can call on at any time for some quick feedback or testing can really help when you have tight deadlines and just need to validate something. Using tools like InVision® and Figma® are quick ways to send prototypes via email and gather quick insights without the need for extensive, time-consuming usability testing. If you're testing users inside the organisation, I've found using Microsoft® Teams® is another quick way to share ideas and get feedback. However, these 'shortcut' tools should only be used once you've built a relationship and the users understand what you're designing.

If the user can't find the product, the user can't buy the product.

Jakob Nielson, PhD and Principal at Nielsen Norman Group

In some of the very large organisations I've worked with, we've often had moments where we don't have time to go to the lengths of recruiting customers and don't have a pool to pull from either. In those situations, we've simply recruited from within the company, finding people who fit the profile.

We've then been able to do quick paper prototype testing within half a day to validate design decisions. I did this with one of the Big 4 banks in Australia, which had a large and diverse pool of staff with varying levels of technology experience. Again, having that trust with a client can really help get the idea of internal testing and paper prototypes over the line.

How failure to usability test cost Citibank® $500m

In 2020, Citibank lost $500 million and suffered a series of rather embarrassing headlines, all because their automated universal core banking software interface, used to make transfers, was confusing—a costly episode that could easily have been avoided if only they had tested on users first and created a more intuitive UI.

What went wrong? Well, Citibank was acting as an agent for Revlon®, which owed hundreds of millions of dollars to various creditors. The company was in the process of refinancing its debt—paying off a few creditors and then rolling the remaining debt into a new loan—and Citibank was tasked with sending out payments totalling $7.8 million. However, a confusing UI resulted in the bank's accidentally paying back the principal on the entire loan, which wasn't due until 2023.

The system required the user to enter the entire amount of the loan into the system and then direct the principal portion of the payment to the 'wash account', which is an internal Citibank account. Figure 4.2 shows what the screen looked like.

The user thought that checking the 'principal' checkbox and entering the number of a Citibank wash account would ensure that the principal payment remained at Citibank. He was wrong. To prevent payment of the principal, the user actually needed to also set the 'front' and 'fund' fields to the wash account.

To further prove the case that the UI was confusing, Citibank had a policy of requiring three people to sign off on a transaction of this size, and all three believed that simply ticking the 'principal' field and entering the wash account number was sufficient. The senior Citibank official even wrote: 'Looks good, please proceed. Principal is going to wash'.

It wasn't until the next day, when the user was conducting a routine review, that they noticed there was something drastically wrong with the previous day's figures. Instead of the intended $7.4 million, they had actually sent out almost $900 million!

Some companies already get the value of design and have designers embedded in teams, design systems in place, continuous loops of usability testing baked into delivery and customer insights driving the priorities of teams in conjunction with the business direction. But there are still many high-profile organisations and large tech companies who not only don't value design but still view it as being visual and someone working in Figma.

Added to this, their design and tech delivery processes are still very 'waterfall', which creates massive inefficiencies and although their products might be highly used the world over, they are bloated and far from intuitive. There are products like the one mentioned in the case study everywhere, and as long as those poorly designed products keep causing adverse events, they fuel the argument for design and the value it gives.

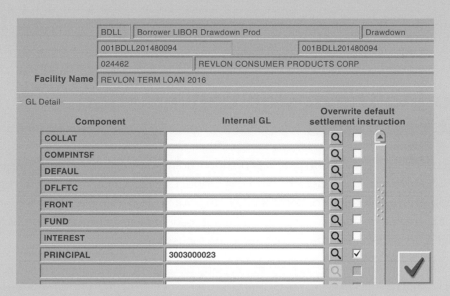

Figure 4.2 Citibank UI 'wash account' screen

Citibank contacted all the creditors to explain the error and ask them to return the overpayment, which some did. However, others refused. In court, Judge Jesse Furman ruled that Citibank wasn't entitled to the return of the outstanding $500 million because the confusion that led to the error was of their own making, through kludgy software and a poorly designed interface. He argued that it was reasonable for the creditors to assume that a bank such as Citibank wouldn't make such a large payment by accident, writing: 'To believe that Citibank, one of the most sophisticated financial institutions in the world, had made a mistake that had never happened before, to the tune of nearly $1 billion—would have been borderline irrational'.

Citibank was given leave to appeal.

On a basic level, if Citibank had simply tested the software with users, they would have discovered any confusing elements. If they had gone a step further, taken a more holistic view and looked at the technology and design together, they could have designed software that was more intuitive and easy to use, with built-in validation alerts or automatically defaulting the principal to wash, and the list goes on . . .

It's a shame that some companies will only recognise the need for design once they've been negatively impacted. As DesignedUp leaders, it's up to us to rise to the challenge and make sure that we succeed in educating those around us about the value of design, helping clients avoid the inevitable pain that comes with underestimating the value design offers. But people love stories—they tend to stay around long after the presentation is over—and we can tell the Citibank story and others like it when talking to clients about the need for early, regular usability testing.

Tailoring the design conversation so it resonates

We can use research, data and usability testing findings to explain the decisions we have made, whether that's determining the product's direction, confirming which interaction is more intuitive or completely ruling out an idea. However, this only shows some of the value design can offer and may not resonate with everyone, especially those who are more numbers and bottom-line focused.

A common problem we face is how to properly determine the real return on a client's investment in design, particularly working in a consultancy, where we don't always get to monitor a product or solution over a long period of time. Success should never be measured on the volume of output or speed, yet many organisations still measure delivery teams simply on how many stories, features or products they churn out.

Success should be measured on value: is the thing we're building going to add value to the customer or users, and how does that positively impact the business in terms of revenue, efficiencies, etc.?

Unfortunately, some businesses simply don't have the baseline data or analytics to track and monitor customers and their experience. Even organisations that have great design teams often don't know the real value they add because the designers don't know how to translate what they do into business language.

So DesignedUp leaders need to translate what they're doing and decisions they've made into a language that resonates with executives in order to help them understand how design impacts their business and bottom line.

This can be done in a number of ways, so you'll need to assess the client and decide which is most appropriate for them—bearing in mind that what is second nature to us as designers is often new to the clients of tech consultancies. But remember that the reason tech consultancies have been buying design agencies and growing their design talent is because they know we provide the missing link between technology and customer experience.

This way of thinking is vital if businesses want to stay relevant. We saw the demise of the once extremely popular Blackberry®, which offered a great solution for people who wanted to work on the go, check and send emails, etc. But they failed to recognise that their customers' needs and problems had changed. When they did react, the technology was buggy, and they provided something that was far less user friendly than other smartphones in the marketplace. Could you imagine living in a world where all the technology you used was created without any consideration of how you as a consumer would actually use it? It would be so frustrating.

Measuring the value of design

We can help others understand design and the value it adds by getting them to be part of the process and experience of how design is really done.

We were helping a large retail brand re-imagine their mobile app and invited execs along to the contextual research sessions we conducted in-store. Experiencing first-hand the many pains of their customers opened their world to having more empathy for them, helping them understand how the app could be completely re-imagined. The result was a team of execs who now understand what design can bring to solving a problem, a deeper connection with their customers and a new app that reached No. 1 on the app store.

However, we can't rely on execs participating in contextual enquiries or expect managers and those who hold the purse strings to be available to attend showcases. So we need to help them understand the value of design in terms of numbers and meeting objectives that align to the business. Businesses need to see a return on their investment, and as designers, we also want to see that our efforts are really solving the problem.

Defining measures of success helps us track and measure our impact and put design in a language that resonates with the business—rather like when we design a solution to be intuitive and resonate with the audience.

> **Design programmes don't teach balanced scorecards—the actual math of ROI. Our business partners struggle to understand that designers don't see the world that way. If designers want a seat at the table, they need to get there.**
>
> Ryan Rumsey, CEO and founder at Second Wave Dive and former Assistant Vice President of Experience Strategy at USAA®

Establishing 'goals' or 'what success looks like' can be hard. Some clients may not have a clear idea themselves of what success looks like, or you may have discovered through early workshops and research that the problem they originally came to you with is not actually the problem they need to solve. Added to this, once goals have been set, not all clients will have solid baseline data to help you track the success. So, as DesignedUp leaders, you'll need to help develop ways to create a baseline measure, such as using customer service call centre data or finding people who can help you get the data—for instance, asking managers to do some guerilla research and track time spent on manual processes over a period of time. Being a good DesignedUp consultant will also mean helping them establish what problem they're actually trying to solve and what the end goal is.

Some clients find it hard to articulate their vision and goals. I was once running a 'What does success look like?' session with a client. They had quite vague requirements, and the original team members weren't very forthcoming. One manager said that they didn't want the new product to launch and have employees who were familiar with the old product refuse to use the new one, which they'd experienced with another internal product. But simply saying: 'I don't want people to refuse to use it' isn't enough of a benchmark for success. We can never guarantee that 100% of users will be happy, especially when some are traditional and have been doing things their way for years. We eventually set some of the goals as:

- Eighty to ninety percent of users would happily move to the new product.
- Reduce the number of data entry errors—the majority of which could be solved through adding validation.
- Make it easy and intuitive enough that current complex calculations that only a mathematician can perform can be done by anyone.
- Reduce the three days required to train staff how to use the product.
- Create a high-performing agile team that the business can use to showcase to other teams and scale.

The items we gathered during the discovery session covered design, tech and the organisation. While it's a good idea to set these at the start of an engagement, they may change over time or be added to as more information is discovered or priorities change.

> ## It's showing how you helped the company either make money or save money.
>
> Heidi Munc, VP of UX, Nationwide®

Your measures of success and the metrics you set need to support your project or product's north star, which also aligns to the business goals. You'll often need to drive these conversations with clients and delve a bit deeper to pull out the right information. The more detailed and solid your goals are, the better you'll be able to respond further down the line, when the business wants to see how successful the new product is.

Ways to measure the value

Forrester has developed a number of reports to help design leaders measure and prove the impact of design. In *The Business Impact Of Design: Five Best Practices For Measuring It**, as the title suggests, they created five essential practices gathered from a variety of both brand and consulting firms:

---

* https://www.forrester.com/report/The-Business-Impact-Of-Design-Five-Best-Practices-For-Measuring-It/RES152255

- Obsess about understanding your stakeholders.
- Focus first on goals, not metrics.
- Know what makes a good metric.
- Don't go it alone.
- Use your design superpowers to bring the numbers to life.

While these are all relevant to both brand and consultancies, they may manifest in slightly different ways. For example, as a design consultant you may only be on a project for a short time and therefore may not be around long enough to collect the numbers. However, building relationships with the stakeholders, focusing on goals and not going it alone are relevant to both in-house designers and consultants, even if you are the only designer on the team.

All designers should be doing the first practice to some degree, depending on their level. As consultants, understanding stakeholders is part of our job—we have to understand who we're dealing with and how to manage and help them.

The second point from the Forrester report—focusing on goals and not metrics—is something that is usually built into any client engagement. The report revealed five of the most common goals that design leaders are trying to achieve:

- Increasing speed to market
- Improving a specific user experience
- Improving a customer journey or the overall customer experience
- Helping the organisation make money or save money
- Changing how people work

Some in-house design teams are siloed away from the business and delivery teams, so different departments often have to be brought together to create these types of goals. This is the same with a consultancy—you have to bring a variety of people together in the first few conversations to create the goals. As consultants, you're coming in from the outside to help the client along on the journey, so your job will be much easier if you can set the expectations at the start, making sure the relevant people are in the room. Whatever it takes, you need to make sure your team creates solid goals for both design and tech and ensure they link back to the business.

If you can link design to the business by presenting your goals and metrics and explaining what your solution(s) will achieve for the business and customer or employee—in showcases, stakeholder meetings and exec meetings—you will gain respect, and people will gradually see the real value design has to offer.

In an interview for their report, Heidi Munc told Forrester: 'Designers often feel like the odd person out at the MBA table. And, unfortunately, without at least a basic understanding of how the firm measures success, design's reach will quickly hit a ceiling'.

Over the years, I have worked with retail, financial services, the public sector, quick-service restaurants, the health sector and the education sector to determine the right problem to solve and setting measures of success. Following is just one example.

What we discovered

Through a series of interviews and workshops with employees across the business and gathering data across several departments, we were able to identify several areas for improvement:

The problem

Seven teams spend time trying to gather the right data using spreadsheets to compensate for inconsistent data across their systems. Marketing wastes the most amount of time—two days per month gathering the right data for their EDMs.

The solution

Synchronising the data across their systems will allow all the teams to look at a single system to understand the customer.

The opportunity

- Save the business two days in wasted employee time every month, allowing employees to focus on higher-value work.
- Provide the customer with a more personal experience, meeting one of the company objectives.
- Prevent customers from having to call the customer service helpline as much as they do today, saving customers and staff time. Reducing unnecessary calls to customer service will enable the team to help customers more in need.

Sometimes the problems you solve will have a far-reaching impact and end up solving a problem for everyone. Matthew Johnston, Head of Disability Inclusion at Thoughtworks, experienced a problem himself as a customer with a hearing impairment:

> I was finding it hard to hear the important announcements at sporting events. After contacting them as a customer, I ended up helping them add captions to the large screens. It helped not only those with hearing loss, but anyone who found it hard to understand the muffled announcements or those whose first language was not English. This helped ensure more people received the important announcements, and everyone had a better experience.

As to the last two recommendations from the Forrester report—'Don't go it alone' and 'Use your design superpowers to bring the numbers to life'—as a design consultant, you may find yourself on a project on your own, but you're still part of a team. It's about bringing all the minds together to help solve the problem. Even if you're with a team of designers, you still need to bring the other minds into the conversation—building great products and services is a team sport. The relationships you build within the organisation as a consultant will help you find the vital information you need when gathering insights and data.

As a consultant, you have to work with what you already have and what you can get your hands on. When it comes to using your design superpowers, if you lean towards being a more research-focused design leader and lack the visual skills to create great presentations, you will have access to more visual designers in your consultancy who might be able to help, and most consultancies have standard templates you can use.

On the other hand, if you're more on the visual side and lack the data and expertise in Excel®, being on a cross-functional team means BAs are your best friends. They can check that your metrics make business sense and can wrangle the data. You can't be the best at everything, so find and use the skills around you to achieve your goal.

Some frameworks to try

There are different ways to define your metrics to track the success and impact of design. You might want to focus more on business metrics or granular success, such as user satisfaction and ease of interaction. Knowing what you want to measure will help you decide which framework works best for you and your team.

There are lots of different approaches and frameworks available—below are a few you can try in workshops with your team and stakeholders. If you want to get more in depth and understand how you can communicate the metrics better with execs and increase your impact by growing an organisation's design maturity, I cover this in detail in the book *DesignedUp at Scale,* which is all about transforming organisations and consultancies into design-centric organisations.

> **As a consultant, you have to work with what you already have and what you can get your hands on.**

RARRA framework

Proposed by Gabor Papp (Technical Program Manager at Meta), this framework relates to retaining customers—something organisations often forget about. COVID-19 forced many organisations to shift their focus towards retaining the customers they would need once they were out the other side of the pandemic while still thinking about what their customers need from them today. It's always easier to sell to existing customers, as they already trust your brand.

The framework focuses on five key areas:

- **Retention.** Do they come back over time?
- **Activation.** What percent have a 'happy' initial experience?
- **Referral.** Do they like it enough to tell their friends?
- **Revenue.** Can you monetise any of this behaviour?
- **Acquisition.** Where/what channels do users come from?

The idea behind this framework is that—due to the quantity of digital products in the consumer market becoming so heavily saturated and competitive—if your product makes a bad first impression, users will probably never come back and may also tell their friends about their bad experience. Providing great value to existing users can fuel organic growth.

As a consultant, you may not be on a project long enough to track this and change the direction; however, you can put the framework and processes in place for the team. You can also use the five areas to help spark initial conversations with the client to identify gaps and find out what success looks like for them. And if you're placed on an existing product that has been running for a few years and is waning in the market, you can implement this framework to track if it improves.

Google's HEART framework

This was developed by the Google research team and applied across the company. It measures user experience on a large scale, such as, when users first test a prototype or the first small release of your product, how did it make them feel? Were they able to successfully complete their task? How many did it without needing you to prompt them? They came up with five categories that can be applied to both the product and feature level:

1. **Happiness.** How people feel about your product (e.g., use the survey to track satisfaction and ease of use).
2. **Engagement.** How people are using your product (e.g., # of 7-day active users, # of users who start a new search per day).
3. **Adoption.** New users (e.g., # of accounts created in the last 7 days).
4. **Retention.** Existing users (e.g., percent of users who use the feature again).
5. **Task success.** Complete actions (e.g., # of users who can accomplish a task).

Increase address search success when placing an online purchase

Goal	Reduce the number of drop-offs after the address search field
Method	Move away from address data and move to location area check
Audience	Customers in all regions
Success criteria	▪ Increase delivery search by 1% will increase sales by 22M
	▪ Gain new customers who previously couldn't buy from us
	▪ Customer complaints on social media regarding not being able to find their address will go down
	▪ App store rating goes up as more people can find their address

Figure 4.3   Example of 'success card'"

This framework can be used to track the success of new products and services and existing products you want to improve. For more long-standing products, you can also use it to track the use of individual features, allowing you to manage the 'bloat' and either remove, improve or replace unused features with something that better solves the user's problem.

Success cards

Another approach is to create 'success cards' to define the goal and what success looks like. You can even add to it, specifying what data you will use to establish a baseline and track the success. These cards can be added to project walls (virtual or physical), confluence and showcase, etc. (see Figure 4.3).

The outcomes

Establishing what success looks like and gathering data to demonstrate you've not only completed the project and mission but that design has made a positive impact on the

* Adapted from 'How to Measure the Impact of Your Work': blog.alexaroman.com/how-to-measure-the-impact-of-your-work-28aad3bcd6cf

business will help change the conversation and the perception of design. As DesignedUp leaders, we already know the huge advantages design can bring; that it touches many areas of an organisation and is vital in decreasing friction across all the customer touchpoints. Following are a few examples across a variety of sectors:

Company: Morrisons, fourth largest grocery retailer in the UK

Design initiative. The traditional re-ordering process at Morrisons was lengthy, manual and prone to error. Five or more employees per store were dedicated to replenishing stock. Staff would print product documents up to 800 pages long and walk the floor to get products on the shelf. Thoughtworks worked with Morrisons to create a more seamless ordering experience for store employees to increase inventory accuracy and allow them to spend more time on the floor helping customers.

Business benefit. The order pad allows data tracking and analysis, higher accuracy, responsive ordering and fewer stockouts. In-store data entry has been reduced by 12 hours per week in each store, and the improved availability has meant a £12 million business benefit. Other existing software the business used would take several days to train people, but the new order pad was so intuitive and easy to use that no training was required, allowing the company to roll it out across 505 stores in 24 weeks. It reduced their training budget and made it easier to train temporary staff over the Christmas season.

> "The order pad strikes at the core of Morrisons business—On-Shelf-Availability. The products that their customers want are on the shelves, no gaps. The design is intuitive for employees, improving accuracy and speed."

Mark Collin, Head of Retail (Europe), Thoughtworks

> The order pad drives us away from having our employees completing administrative tasks in the store. It gives them more time to be on the shop floor, working near our customers

Richard Manners, Retail Improvement Director, Morrisons

$80,000,000

The value of colour #0044CC

Figure 4.4 The blue that earnt Microsoft $80 million in revenue

Company: Microsoft

Design initiative. Significantly improve the click rate of call-to-action links on Bing® by testing a vast number of colours to see which users engaged with the most and ffered the best contrast.

Business benefit. Changing the links to the pacific shade of blue (#0044CC) (see Figure 4.4) over other hues added an additional $80 million in annual revenue.

Company: Uber

Design initiative. Spent time learning what customers were doing on their landing page. Addressed a number of visual issues impacting cognitive load and preventing users from quickly finding the information they needed. For insight into the use of RealEye.io eye-tracking heat maps in the redesign, see Figures 4.5 and 4.6 (on next pages), and visit https://uxplanet.org/how-uber-changed -its-main-page-to-optimize-conversion-investigated-with-eye-tracking-tool -e4241b347e3d

Business benefit. Three times more attention was given to 'sign up' buttons after addressing the visual issues.

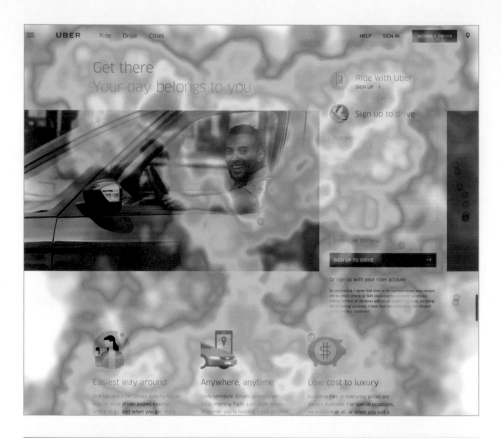

Figure 4.5 RealEye Heat Map before (top), and after (bottom) (Eye-tracking heatmap generated using webcam eye-tracking platform: www.realeye.io; used with permission)

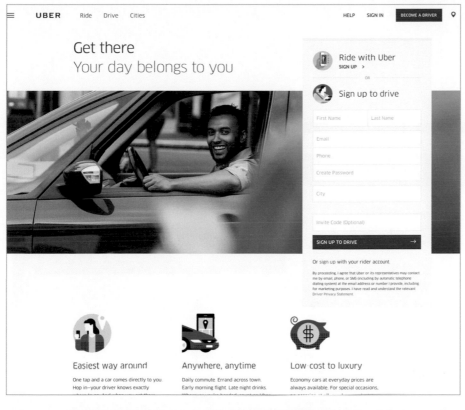

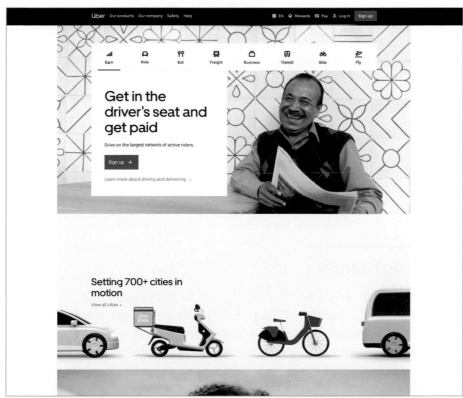

Figure 4.6 Uber landing page before (top), and after (bottom)
(Images used with permission of Uber Technologies, Inc.)

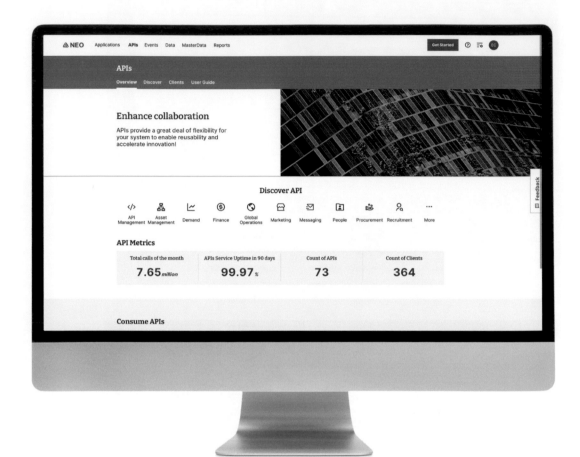

Figure 4.7   (This and next page) Self-serve portal for developers
(Images used with permission of Thoughtworks, Inc.)

Company: Thoughtworks

Design initiative. Built a self-serve portal for developers for discovering and consuming core digital assets after diagnosing that it took two to three weeks to provision infrastructure, processes were not well defined, tools and applications were hard to find and there was a lack of visibility of delivery metrics. Through user research and applying human-centred design, the cross-functional team designed and built a new developer platform (NEO) (see Figure 4.7).

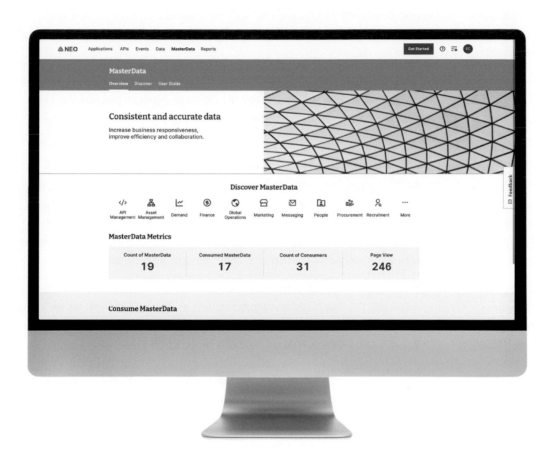

Business benefit. The development cycle was significantly improved, with 90% of waste removed from iteration '0', and developer effectiveness was improved by 20–30%, contributing to Thoughtworks' operational efficiency and efficiency of clients' projects. Self-serve onboarding and offboarding of team members and full discoverability of core assets (475+ applications, 70+ APIs, 410 events, 70+ dashboards) dramatically improved the developer experience. The new platform went on to win the Foundry's CIO 100 Award, placing Thoughtworks among 'The Most Innovative IT Organisations'.

Showing the continuous value of design

DesignedUp leaders, especially those on delivery teams, are continually seeking feedback on ideas and solutions to ensure the right outcome is achieved. We love solving problems no matter how large or small—we want to make an impact and make something better than it was.

Feeding your findings from research and usability testing back to the business, not just within your team, allows you to demonstrate how design has uncovered the real problem that needs solving; how design and tech working together has solved the problem, and what impact that has had on the customer, product success and business.

Don't present all your findings; tailor them to the audience and align them to the metrics, product and the organisation's north star. Throughout the product's lifecycle and evolution, you'll continually uncover new things in usability testing and will need to decide (a) if they're a priority and (b) how much they impact your current goals, budget, timeline and customer experience. There is always ebb and flow in this process, especially when you're working with customers, tech, design and business.

If you're presenting to execs or a board of directors, be selective in what you show because they are often only interested in the high-level information and results: 'What value is this giving the business?' and 'Does this help us get closer to meeting our vision?' For example, the narrative could be: 'We discovered 20% of the calls made to the call centre are from customers who need their passwords reset. To solve this, in the new software we've designed and tested an easy way for customers to self-serve and reset their password. This will reduce the number of calls and free up the staff to focus on the more critical ones'.

Presenting this allows those who make the decisions about budgets to start understanding the value of design and that it's not just something visual—it has tangible business benefits.

> **Companies in our study reported that when design takes centre stage, it can have a direct impact on tangible business results, like revenue, valuation, and time to market.**
>
> The New Design Frontier Report, 2019[*]

Tracking a product's usability over time allows us to gather data to ensure the product is staying relevant, to continually track the metrics to see how much we've nudged the needle or completely shifted the experience, and the impact that's had on the business and the customers. Feeding back to the business that you have found an appropriate

---

[*] https://www.invisionapp.com/design-better/design-maturity-model/

baseline and have implemented ways to track progress will help you change the conversation from 'design . . . blah blah blah' to something that resonates.

Putting these types of initiatives in place—or, at the very least, discussing them—is one sign you're going from thinking like a designer to thinking like a DesignedUp leader. You are now thinking beyond just design.

The time you have available, your budget and the size of your team will also impact how you capture the data over time. Some organisations will have analytic tools built into their products, with departments tracking various metrics regarding the customer—such as most common call enquiries, sales, leading and failing product lines—all of which give you insights. Coupling this data with usability testing and the various ways of gaining customer feedback will help you create a compelling narrative when presenting your findings and prioritising what's next.

As a consultant, you'll need to decide with the team what data capture method works best and make sure there's someone who can take ownership of it once you leave. If it's something like an analytics tool, you'll need to have another analytically minded person on the team that can handle it—perhaps the BA or PM. If you're not analytically minded yourself, you could pair with a BA on this task.

Google Analytics, Adobe® Analytics and Mixpanel® are all products that teams use to track user behaviour. Some products are event based (unlike Google Analytics, which is page based); the advantage of tracking an 'event' being that you can see the discrete interactions a user has with a

> **Linking your design work to business impact will help you be seen as not *just* a designer.**

product—for example, 'viewed booking' or 'booked a flight'—and that level of detail is really useful once your product is launched or has been in the market for a while.

Some event-based tools allow you to see individual user paths and how they navigate through, moment by moment. Be aware that certain tools may require extra code to be added during the build stage, so you'll need to factor this in, especially if you're retrofitting or decide to delay adding analytics at the start of a new product.

You can also use surveys or collect perception-based metrics about ease of use and findability. Whatever your method for capturing data, the most important thing is that you share it with your team, the organisation and the consultancy you work for, so that it's clear to everyone the value design brings and helps them better understand their customers. You can also use your data findings to highlight areas where you might need to bring specific expertise onto the project, or show how you could do more if you had more designers in a certain field to help.

This whole process may not sound very interesting or creative, but linking your work back to the business will help you with prioritising tasks. For example, I was on a government 'change review' process, where any extra or new items that were tech or design related would be discussed and prioritised. This involved adding a valid reason for the item to the storycard, saying: 'The research found this, so we'd like to do this to solve the problem. We've tested the idea and it worked. Building this will reduce and enable this. It's recommended that this be added to phase X of the project'.

Gathering findings and showing the impact a solution has had—even if the product hasn't launched into the market yet—enables you to ensure you're on track to achieve the overall vision and meet the business objectives. It will also help the developers and the rest of the team understand what design can achieve.

While it's important to track the success of the work you're doing, you also need to define goals for yourself and track your own performance, which you can then feed into pay and performance reviews. What goals do you have as the designer on the project and within the consultancy? Is it improving your leadership skills to influence, upskilling in a new area, such as accessibility? Many consultancies and agencies have their own ways to track and gather feedback, and you may have a mentor who can help you set goals for the year.

Use your successes metrics to influence sales

Sales is something many designers shy away from, but to get design a seat at the top table, you need to become good friends with the sales team, especially in a tech consultancy. This will allow you access to early conversations about design, where you can sow the seed about its importance and the value it brings. You can start by helping the sales team with proposals, and rather than just making their deck pretty, take the opportunity to help them create something that is more empathetic to the target audience and tells the story in a better way.

Building these relationships will eventually lead to your being involved in initial conversations with the client, where you'll gain a deeper understanding of the problem they're trying to solve and can talk directly to them about the value of design how it will help create the best solution to their problem. Sometimes, you might have to question the approach they're proposing and present an alternative solution that they may not have thought of or heard about (which is why they're speaking to you!).

Again, back up your case for design with data. Use stats to show the positive impact of having a designer on the project at the very beginning. It could be that the client wants to scale by improving inefficiencies in their teams' processes, rather than hiring more employees; however, they don't know what areas need to be improved or where the main pain points are. Having designers, specifically researchers, as part of the discovery phase will help quickly identify what the real problem is and bring the humans it impacts into the conversation. Use past examples to support your reasoning, such as the one mentioned earlier about saving two days per month of wasted time within a marketing team by improving the transparency and accuracy of their data.

It could be that the client views design as simply making something pretty, so explain that visual design affects user behaviour and the overall product experience, reducing visual stress by speeding up the processing power of the brain, which is really important when 65% of the population are visual learners.

If the client is launching a new digital product, explain that they have just 50 milliseconds before a user has made their first judgements. Quote examples such as: Hotel Tonight were able to reduce failed bookings by 75% by introducing an antipattern; Bing invested time testing the optimum blue hue, which resulted in an additional $80 million in annual revenue; Google are continuously testing link colours so they can optimise performance.

So, in summary . . .

Every consultant has to take the stakeholders and team along on the design journey to understand what design really is, how it works and the value it adds. It could involve taking them through an organisational transformation, helping them shape and grow high-performing product teams or guiding them through unpacking, defining and creating a clear approach to solving their problem.

Design leadership within a consultancy is the same—we have to take the consultancy along on the journey and help them understand what design is—but we also have to help them truly understand its value and power at the same time. To demonstrate that effectively, DesignedUp leaders inside a consultancy have to back up their decisions with the kind of data and evidence that resonates at a business level.

There is, however, a balance—we don't want to get so fixated on metrics and conforming to business goals that we forget about the humans and prevent ourselves from having the space to think creatively and innovate. Becoming metric obsessed will kill the designer within us.

With every client comes a new team and new challenges, and you have to embrace this and see it as another opportunity to change the perception of design in the wider business world.

Little by little, if we persevere, we will transform the thinking of organisations so that they always view their products and solutions from a customer perspective and appreciate the tangible value of design. As DesignedUp leaders, if we can leave our clients in a better position than we found them and make life easier for the next designer coming in, our work is done.

don't become the worst version of yourself

While designers will always be in the minority in the tech industry, there is no reason why the ratio of male to female design leaders shouldn't be more balanced. Having more women in leadership roles positively impacts both men and women, yet it's rarely talked about. No matter where your career takes you, you'll encounter the one percent who will challenge you. In this chapter we discuss what is at the root of certain attitudes and behaviours, how the largest contextual enquiry has changed some of those systemic beliefs and why it should be about the right person for the job, regardless of who they are.

a s you progress on your journey to leadership, stay true to who you are, be empathic and authentic, and don't feel the need to conform to societal stereotypes. Being at the top of your game may appear to others as glamorous, but it can be a lonely place and sometimes a toxic environment where the loudest or most narcissistic person is the one who gets heard. Smooth-talking individuals without any real substance will manage to pass off other people's ideas as their own, become friends with the inner circle of influence and rise up through the ranks. Some eventually get found out; others continue to pull it off for years.

But while we can sit back in disbelief that this kind of thing happens—and we don't and shouldn't want to become like these people—it is worth looking at how they act in different situations to see if there are any particular takeaways that we can learn to help us progress. Remember, you don't need to become the worst version of yourself to reach all the way to the top.

The tech industry has a bad reputation for not supporting females—especially those who want to progress into leadership. However, this is starting to change, and more and more women, men and organisations are becoming comfortable with calling out bad behaviour. However, while the focus has been on female role models and helping women to rise up through the ranks, we can't forget our male counterparts. Just as design and tech need to work together, we all—men, women, gay, trans, gender neutral, however you define yourself—need to help and support one another to realise our full potential. Whatever happens as we progress our careers, we must always strive to be the best possible version of ourselves and not get lost in the scramble to the top. That said, it doesn't mean we should just sit back and wait for leadership to come to us; we need to push for what we want and what we believe in, say yes to opportunities, be unapologetic—while remaining a decent human being.

Dealing with conflicting attitudes

I have dealt with my fair share of sexism throughout my career, but I'm lucky that Thoughtworks® is very inclusive and forward thinking, as are many other consultancies and tech companies. However, being a consultant means you will be working with clients who may not be as forward thinking. You could see yourself going from an inclusive organisation to occasionally finding yourself reliving the past. As a design leader in a consultancy, while you're helping clients realise the value of design, you may also need to be strong enough to call out systemic sexist attitudes and other bad behaviour where you encounter it—for the good of everyone both on the team and in the wider organisation.

Sometimes you meet people who make you wonder what their past was like and whether, if they were to do some self-reflection and soul searching, they would change. You will never know what's really going on in someone's life, especially if you're a consultant, as you're somewhat removed from their internal politics and office gossip—and the majority of the time that's a good thing! However, when managing stakeholders, it's especially important to understand what's driving them—the pressures they're under, their fears and who their allies or drinking buddies are. It's hard to understand some people's agendas, and you will probably never change their bad behaviour or find out what past experience or trauma might be driving them to behave in a certain way; however, even if you don't call it out in the moment because you're not prepared to die on that hill, it's vital that you have a company and a team that support you and have your back.

We were helping a client re-imagine a dated digital product and were several weeks into working onsite as a cross functional team when the client employed a new product owner, let's call him Bill, who became one of our main stakeholders. His background was in some really interesting sectors of the tech industry, and the client was hoping he'd inject some innovation into their organisation based on his past experience. Quite the opposite happened—he turned out to be incompetent and lacking in vision and ideas. In addition, he displayed an attitude of male dominance and sexism.

His behaviour was first noticed in a stakeholder standup. On this particular day, the main stakeholders, with whom we had a great relationship, weren't around, and neither was our project manager. Our tech lead, the lead developer and I were running the session; I was the only female, and Bill was the only one from the client organisation attending. The tech lead and lead developer walked the wall with Bill and then passed to me to walk through the design and research section of the wall. Nothing unusual about the process until it was handed to me, and then the stakeholder started picking holes in the way it was presented on the wall. I answered all his questions around the customer research process and justified everything. After the meeting, the lead developer remarked that Bill had spoken differently to me, and I have to say, I appreciated having someone on the team call it out.

This became a common theme—Bill would often be rude and patronising to senior females on our team, notably when they were either on their own with him or there was no one else from the client present. As a consultant, you never know what situation you're going to walk into, and when you're based at clients' offices, some behaviours that would not be tolerated by your employer can sometimes go unnoticed.

Situations like these have to be handled in the correct way, which is where having the support of your team and the company you work for is crucial. It's a good idea to keep a log of 'risks' as a team—these can be general project risks you openly share with the client; risks that you keep internal (such as with this person); a process the client uses to sign off on work, their production process or ways of working with designers. Keeping a log of risks helps you prepare and plan for every eventuality.

In this case, once we noticed a pattern, we raised our concerns with the account handler. The team had kept a log of the incidents—times and dates—which the account handler later shared with the client. Although we acted quickly and Thoughtworks were completely supportive of us, it took awhile for our client to see that not only did Bill treat the female consultants on our team this way, he also treated their longstanding female staff the same way. He no longer works at the company.

Dr Andy Polaine spent many years working at Fjord® as the Global Group Design Director of Client Evolution and is the co-author of the book *Service Design: From Insight to Implementation,* among many other things. He and I were discussing how women can lead inside male-dominated tech companies without being seen as the 'aggressive female'. For those of you who don't know, Andy also hosts the 'Power of Ten' podcast and coaches many leading female designers.

Andy's very honest and open point of view draws on the fact that we need allyship on both sides of the fence—both men and women need to step up:

> Take all the classic approaches of, 'Oh, hang on a second, I think Emma wanted to say something', or 'Didn't Emma already say what you just said?' to counteract mansplaining. I hate to say it—and I'm certainly not being an apologist for men who really do need to change their behaviour—but one of the reasons men can be great allies is precisely because mansplaining men listen to other men. If a man calls out the mansplaining or domination of the conversation, it is received differently and lands differently to when a woman is calling it out. When women call it out, it's easy to trigger the negative responses of, 'You're just nagging, bitching, aggressive, etc'.—all those pejoratives that aren't there for men. So, men (especially white, middle-aged men) can use their privilege in a positive way and be allies to women in that environment.

So, while we women need more female figures to look up to, and they need to be our allies and cheerleaders, we also need to build relationships with, support and be supported by our male co-workers. This is particularly important in the tech consulting world, where you will find yourself among a lot of men—it's really about being a team.

In consulting, you never know when you're going to turn up at a client and be faced with a room full of men who have never spoken to a customer or taken a human-centred approach in their lives. Individually, they really care about their work and want to create something great, but a lack of leadership has resulted in their working against one another, and the team has fallen apart. So, you have to fix the team before you dive into the value of design, otherwise you'll be dealing with a manager who treats you differently because you're a female, and even if you brush it off, the other men on your team will notice it.

Cassandra Kelsall is the Director of Experience at Publicis Sapient. She has experienced mansplaining first-hand in a leadership environment, which she feels could partly be due to the fact that she isn't always as succinct in explaining her ideas as she would like; however, owing to the team culture, they were able to turn it into a bit of harmless banter:

> I tend to think out loud as I'm working through my ideas, as opposed to considering them and then making my point. My colleague was a chronic mansplainer, yet he had a complete lack of awareness that he was doing it. We were lucky at the time that the leadership team was close to half women, which certainly made a difference in having a sense of backup and others to call out small behaviours like that which chip away over time.

> A female colleague pointed it out at one meeting where it was plain as day, but in a light way so as not to make him feel bad. And then we started to call it out by flipping it, like, 'Sorry, was I on mute? Did you just say what I was saying?' Changing deep-seated behaviours starts with self-awareness and really knowing how to sense and respond.

Andy interviewed Katja Forbes, Head of Client Experience at CCIB DCDA in

The standard you walk past is the standard you accept.*

* Lieutenant-General David Morrison, Australian Chief of Army (Rtd.).

Singapore and a member of the Global Board of the Interaction Design Association, about her journey into design leadership. She talks about the energy it takes to 'fight the fight' as a female and refers to the quote from Lieutenant-General David Morrison, Australian Chief of Army (Rtd.), 'The standard you walk past is the standard you accept'.

During the interview, Katja recalls her first memories of having the confidence to call out when something wasn't right.

> I was living in London and working for Sapient at the time, working with an English bank on a fairly tech-heavy project. I was running the project and all its facets and had called a meeting where there were lots of people from the tech side and business side in the room. A man from the bank sat next to me and said, 'Oh, are you going to take some minutes?' And I thought: I am not having this. This was the first time I could remember calling out that kind of sexist attitude.

> I said, 'Why? Is it because I'm the only woman in the room?' And it was really satisfying to watch him curl up like a slug I'd put salt on. I said, 'I will take notes for myself, but I'm not here for the minute taking. I'm here to facilitate the session, that's my job here'. I don't fight every battle; I think in terms of fatigue, you have to decide which hills are worth dying on, because sometimes it's just not worth it'.

I asked Andy what he thought about calling out bad behaviour. He said, 'I'm a big fan of naming behaviour. It's a bit of a risky strategy—you have to be relatively self-confident to do it in the first place—but it is really helpful and worthwhile, because it makes the behaviour visible to those in the room who may not have noticed it'.

When talking to Mariel Macia, Senior Service Design Manager at McKinsey & Company®, about her career as a female designer, she reported having experienced what Kimberlé Crenshaw, professor at the UCLA School of Law and Columbia Law School, coined 'intersectionality', which is a form of discrimination that takes different aspects of a person's social identity and exposes them to overlapping forms of discrimination and marginalisation. She has found people to be more negative towards her nationality rather than her being female. She would often get people asking how she can design for their customers when her nationality is different, to which she would respond, 'Through user research and speaking to the customers'.

Often, such as during sales pitches, clients will ask what you can bring to the team if you don't have experience in their particular field. As design leaders, we need to explain how we overcome these problems and the advantage to having a diverse perspective.

It's examples like these that make you wonder if the attitudes are systemic; do they come from childhood—did they simply not have the right role models? Were they exposed to bad behaviours in previous companies, leading them to believe that's the way to get ahead? Whatever it is, we need to either call it out in the moment, raise it as a risk to the project, or raise it to the companies we work for. One voice can often go unheard, but if we can all be committed as a team to calling out bad behaviour and backing each other up, we can start to change both the companies we work for and the people we work with.

Ian Kelsall, Principal of Product Management at Thoughtworks®, has observed that:

> Younger male designers, both within Thoughtworks and at clients, tend to be far more cognisant of imposing their opinion on a group with a much more consultative and empathetic approach than previous generations of male designers may have felt they needed to portray in order to be taken seriously. I anticipate there may be a slew of more self-conscientious younger male designers who are less inclined to assume leadership positions.

The 1%

While organisations are certainly trying to change outdated attitudes and eliminate bad behaviours, you will inevitably come across a tiny minority of people who challenge you, and as Katja said, you need to decide which hill you're willing to die on. It's also worth remembering that sometimes it's a generational thing—some people have spent the majority of their working lives in male-dominated organisations, which leads them to behave in a particular way, or it's just the way they have been brought up.

So sometimes you just need to brush off comments where you know no harm was intended. If we start to get offended by every comment, we're in danger of turning our workplaces into areas where people can't be themselves and we can no longer have fun banter for fear of offending someone.

There will be times where you need to go around the person and avoid tackling them directly—as mentioned earlier, where we kept an incident log. And there will also be times where you don't always know the internal relationships and have to navigate the right path.

In the early years of building my design agency in the UK, when I was around 27, we'd been working with a large new client for around eight months, and everything was going well. We'd established a great relationship, and they loved all the work. They then employed a general manager, let's call him 'John'. John would consistently divert questions away from me and towards my marketing person—who happened to be male and older than I was—even though I was the owner of the company and the one driving projects.

John then took it upon himself to go through every invoice we'd ever issued, despite the work having been completed and delivered on time, and all the invoices already paid in full. He was scrutinising areas he knew little about, which resulted in a meeting with him where I had to justify everything we had completed over the eight months before he joined the company.

He was incredibly rude and difficult to work with in the meeting. He then refused to pay a recent and substantial invoice, where the quote had been approved prior to his joining. The work had been completed on time, within budget, and he'd witnessed first-hand the successful outcome of the project in question. The two founders were really happy with the work we'd achieved and the great results. Having them not pay would have had large implications for my business, as it involved work completed by several of our longstanding suppliers, who also needed paying.

I tried to resolve the issue directly with John but to no avail. I had a good relationship with the company's founders—let's call them 'Alex' and 'Steve'—although a slightly better relationship with Alex. Unfortunately, Alex was away on holiday at the time, so I spoke to Steve—who I didn't know was actually best friends with John. (It's times like this when knowing the internal relationships of your stakeholders is helpful!) Steve told me to speak to John and washed his hands of the entire situation.

I was not one to give up, knowing I was right and had a winning case if it resulted in our going to court. When Alex returned from holiday, I spoke to him, and he said: 'I'm sorry, he treats everyone like they're a utility supplier and thinks he can push everyone down on price. Send me the invoice when he's on holiday next week, and I'll get it paid without his knowing'. Alex paid it the following week, but what does that say about the company when a founder has to go behind the back of someone they had employed?

Soon after this, Alex and Steve sold the company. Over coffee while I was helping Alex with his new business venture, he said it wouldn't have changed anything no matter how I'd handled John, he was just that sort of person. He shared with me that John had actually been dismissive towards Alex's wife!

There will always be those '1%-ers' who challenge us, and however we choose to deal with their behaviour—whether we call it out in the moment or go around them to get the desired result—as long as we are learning, we are growing and can use those experiences to help us with similar situations in the future.

I learnt very early on in my business journey to act swiftly with clients who were showing particular traits that could lead to unpaid invoices, projects blowing out, etc. I also learnt how the law worked and didn't hesitate the moment I could see the signs a client thought they could walk all over me. I wouldn't hold back on putting their accounts on stop until they had paid or issuing them with the relevant paperwork to take them to court. If a potential client didn't like the price, I was willing to walk away because I valued the work we did.

Luckily, this didn't happen very often, and we had some incredible, forward-thinking clients whom we worked with for years. In life there will always be that 1%-er who just likes to ruin your day—we simply need to pick ourselves up, learn how we could do things differently next time and move on. Your life experiences—often some of the most difficult and challenging ones—will help you become a better consultant and leader.

Our past relationships influence us—sometimes unknowingly

Throughout our lives, we are constantly learning and being shaped by moments that happen to us and around us. These can affect not only how we behave towards others but how we respond to other people's attitudes towards us. Often while conducting customer interviews, designers uncover moments that have shaped people, gaining extra insights into customers' psyches. Having empathy for other people and the ability to see the multitude of possibilities as to why someone could be reacting in a particular way allows us to learn and adopt approaches to help us communicate better with others. And while we need to understand how our stakeholders and customers think and feel, it's important to also look back on our own past to understand why we might be reacting in a particular way.

When Andy coaches designers, he often talks to them about their relationships with parents and teachers because these are usually our first experiences with someone who's in charge. He's found that people often end up relating to their boss or colleagues —particularly their boss—with a kind of parental dynamic. In one particular case, he was coaching a really smart and intelligent woman who was struggling with her boss's micro-managing. Looking back on her past, she realised that she was responding to her boss like she did to her stepmother when she was a teenager. Even though she has a great relationship with her stepmum now, her boss's behaviour was triggering a particular reaction, unearthing emotions from when she was younger, so her emotional response was much more magnified than you would expect it to be.

In Colleen Callander's book *Leader by Design,* she reflects on her childhood and how it shaped the path to her becoming the CEO of the women's clothing line Sportgirl. Her hardworking mum was a people pleaser had always said yes, and she watched her dad grow his own very successful building company. While these influences helped her progress with her career, the desire to always want to please others resulted in her taking on far too much later in her career, which started to negatively affect her and her family. She has learnt from this and has now changed her approach to managing her time to ensure she has a better balance.

My own parents were very supportive of my crazy design ideas, which I'd often discuss with them, usually while perched on the kitchen table as my mum cooked dinner. They would always help me with my problem solving, even coming back to me a few days later saying, 'I've been thinking about your problem, what about . . .' I guess this is where my need to problem solve in every situation has come from. And, like Colleen, I am learning not to say yes to everything!

My mum was also keen for me to never be afraid to speak up for myself, always telling me, 'They're only human', and, 'If you don't ask you don't get'—but this is not the case for everyone. Often you are told that you shouldn't ask certain questions and you have to be the quiet one—for sure, if my sisters and I were making noise, my gran would say, 'Children should be seen and not heard!' All these influences affect us on a personal level, and Andy thinks this is magnified if you're a designer:

> In design in general, we have this idea that's a socialised thing from school, where designers are the kids and the suits are the adults. In my experience, it has been the opposite—most people in design are far more emotionally mature than people who have spent their whole lives in corporate spaces rather than places with 'playground-like' creativity.

We don't always know what is going on in someone else's life, what 'moments' have shaped them or what pressures they might be under at work and home. However, we can all do some self-reflection and think about whether our reaction to a particular situation might be due to our past. Once we've identified the 'source' of our response, we can work on adapting and improving it.

Because we designers like to experiment, Andy encourages the people he mentors to try different approaches to situations or reframe things to see what happens and what the reaction is. 'I'll get back to you' is one he urged a lady he was coaching to use. Despite being switched on and smart, she was nervous and worried about not knowing all the answers during a presentation and would often become a 'deer in the headlights'. Using 'I'll get back to you' allows you to take the time to form a more considered view or gather more in-depth details. This helped Andy's coachee become less nervous and gave her the opportunity to give greater clarity with her answer.

Say 'yes', then figure it out later

While not all women struggle with self-confidence, it seems to be much more common for women to put themselves down, suffer self-doubt and not step forward for opportunities unless they are 100% confident. Not everyone wants to be a leader, and many men and women are comfortable being the 'doers', but if we are going to increase the number of female design leaders, we need to start feeling more comfortable saying yes and figuring it out later. What's the worst that can happen? Even if you fail, you'll learn a lot in the process.

When I asked some of the male designers I know if they ever doubt their abilities, Joshua Kinal, Experience Design lead at Thoughtworks, shared some good and bad examples of what he has witnessed:

> I've seen many male designers never doubt their abilities and lash out when they are challenged. However, the strongest creatives I've worked with were the ones who would be open to takedowns: 'Tell me why this design [I've come up with] doesn't work' can be a good authoritative starting point—it opens with vulnerability as a leadership trait.

He referred to this as 'doubting with confidence' and went on to give me an example of another male designer who didn't need to express doubt or vulnerability to be different from the others. 'He is naturally welcoming and encouraging and got where he is because his interest is in design and its tools, not himself'.

During Cassandra's 10 years at Sapient, she has seen the company undergo many transformations—starting in tech, acquiring creative and management consulting capability, and being acquired by a global holding group. She has built a strong experience design team and is very proud that she has a large number of female leaders within her team. I asked what differences, if any, she has noticed between male and female designers. She has seen with all levels of designers that men tend to exuberate in their abilities, and she has seen some women who are very clear on where they want to be and want they want. However:

> The majority of conversations I've had around remuneration have been driven by male employees demanding to be compensated comparatively higher for their contributions. They are generally better at presenting the case for merit increases, tracking the market and their contributions and documenting the impact they've had, speaking confidently—sometimes over-confidently—about their competencies.

> That's an area where women need more support. I have a couple of female rockstars who are continually recognised by peers, clients and award nominations, yet they're consistently more humble. Recognising and celebrating people is a core aspect of culture; it's something I encourage and I see coming both from males and females across the team, but it takes a proactive people manager to advocate for those who may not come forward or be forthright about compensation.

> This might be an over-generalisation, but over the years I've found that males do tend to be more direct—they say, 'I've hit all my targets, I want a pay rise', whereas women tend to have the conversation around wanting to know where they sit and if there are gaps they need to close to achieve that next threshold.

She has also observed that women who come from the management consulting world are more direct in their approach to climbing the career ladder, whereas women from the design industry orient to impact and progression in a different way; however, those edges appear to be blurring as design has become a more transactional than vocational pathway.

> I had one very talented young woman who was incredibly assertive, and it was actually refreshing. A few months into the role, she was already saying, 'Once I'm eligible after 12 months I want that promotion. Tell me what else I need to do? Otherwise I expect it to go through, and by the way I want this much money'. I'm, like, Wow! It's unusual, but for that younger cohort in an employee's market, I certainly think it's indicative of a new wave of entitlement we're starting to see across more junior designers.

While Cassandra has seen a difference between the male and females on her team, there are introverts and extroverts across both genders. The largest difference in traits and approaches to pay conversations and career seems to be driven by their background. Ian Kelsall doesn't see himself as a designer, but more an analyst who is good at seeing and presenting broader context and who is a strong advocate of design to solve things in new ways. Ian always comes across as articulate and confident, yet he says:

> As an introvert who can present as an extrovert, I constantly feel underprepared, out of my depth and exhausted. However, I try not to let that prevent my having hard conversations and being direct when I need to. I see self-doubt as a useful tool to help me reflect, but it shouldn't stop my moving forward and improving. Gaining confidence is a pattern of behaviour for me, and I need to practice avoiding becoming too introspective.

Many women doubt themselves, think they're not good enough or fear they will be found out—it's that pesky Impostor Syndrome again! We need to stop doubting ourselves and to say yes to opportunities when they arise. If an opportunity exists that helps you towards your goal or has the potential to open new doors, take it, even if it scares you. The opportunity might only present itself to you once. One of my male colleagues had put forward two women he felt deserved a promotion, yet when he told them, they said they weren't comfortable with this, as they felt they weren't ready—they wanted to wait until the next round of promotions and reassess it then.

But there may not be another round, or the person who put you forward this time might move job or company, which could potentially leave you without an advocate next time. Grab every opportunity that comes your way—because if you don't, someone else will. Andy Polaine has coached many women through challenges they've faced. During our chat he stated:

> [Women need to] believe that making it up is fine. When you move into a leadership position, your job is to kind of make stuff up as you're going along. There's not always a script for it, because that's the whole point—otherwise, you would be following someone else. If you've been socialised to believe that women have to do what they're told and follow the rules, then it's a real challenge because the messaging you've received is, 'if you screw up, it's because you're a woman'; it's not because you made a choice and it didn't turn out like you thought. You need a sense of self-confidence and to build up the resilience against that kind of messaging.

Cassandra added this:

> One of the things that always stands out to me—and I say it to junior team members a lot, and when seniors go into lead level—is that everyone else is making it up. There's a point at which you reach a threshold and you have to jump over the abyss, and then once you land at the big table, you realise that all the people sitting around it are making it up as they go along. But they're confident in doing

it—they're willing to put their necks on the line and have the courage of their convictions; to give it a go and be accountable to that outcome.

As a principle for anyone who is lacking that confidence, I always say: remember that people don't know what you don't know. Whether it's a pitch or a presentation at a conference, it's highly unlikely that your audience know what you meant to say or what you forgot.

So, trust your instincts and roll with it. You need to believe in yourself, that if you are smart, passionate and work hard, the outcome will be good, but it's your own responsibility to drive that outcome as a leader. As a consultant, we're all only five minutes ahead of the client. People learn methods, tools and practices from everywhere, add a pinch of their own creativity and put themselves out there—half the time it may fail, and you've got to be okay with that.

Sometimes opportunities arise at unexpected times, and you say yes where many other women would have said no. In early 2016, I was one year into my new job at Thoughtworks, trying to navigate being a designer inside a tech consulting firm, when I became pregnant with my first child. Shortly after I found out, I was selected to be part of the Thoughtworks 18-month Global Leadership Development Programme, which would entail travel not only before I was due, but also a few weeks after. I could have said no and turned down the opportunity, but that just isn't me—I don't like to do things by half—so I said yes. There is always a way to make something work, and it's far better to try than have regrets over missing out.

It was Ryan Moffat, the MD of Thoughtworks Australia at the time, who had called to tell me the exciting news that I'd been selected—only two people were selected from each country for the programme, and I was one of Australia's two! I had known from day one of joining the company that I wanted to have more impact globally and progress my career, and in the back of my mind, I was worried the opportunity would be taken away once I said I was pregnant.

My husband and I had talked a lot about if and when we might have children. He knew I was a career girl—it's why he liked me in the first place—and he also knew that my biggest fear was losing everything I'd worked hard for. Although I recognised that having a baby would change our lives, I didn't want it to end my career. Some may say this is selfish, but I'd worked too hard to give it all up, and I love what I do. We agreed we'd always make it work, somehow, and I firmly believe showing my children that you need to work at what you want to achieve will make them better people.

After the call with Ryan, I was so excited and rang my husband to tell him the news. He asked me if I'd told Ryan I was pregnant. When I said no, he told me I needed to, and said, 'If they're not going to support you, then they're not the company you want to work for'. He had a point. I could have called Ryan back and handed him a potential problem. But instead, in my problem-solving, solution-oriented designer style, I called back to tell him out of courtesy and to reassure him that everything was going to work with my dates and I already had a plan. Was I worried he'd turn round and say that my situation changes everything? Of course! And the reaction from some of my friends confirmed my concerns: 'I bet when you told him you were pregnant he kicked himself for selecting you, especially as you're going to cost the business lots of money'. Instead, Ryan congratulated me on the news and went on to tell me about how his wife had started a business when she was on maternity leave.

Our final face-to-face workshop was held in Melbourne, and I flew down with my seven-week-old baby. My husband couldn't come with me due to last-minute work obligations, but luckily my father-in-law was visiting from the UK and travelled with me until my husband could join us. James, my now six-year-old, has travelled more as an unborn baby than in his six years on land!

I went on to complete the Leadership Programme and was the first person in the company who had completed it while pregnant (see Figure 5.1). This then led to somewhat of a trend, with other pregnant women or new mums taking part in the years that followed, and I became a coach on the programme when one of my coachees had a newborn.

Figure 5.1   Emma and James with the 2016 Global Technology Leadership Development Programme team (Image used with permission of Thoughtworks, Inc.)

After my experience, lots of women approached me wanting to know how I did it. This led to my writing an article titled, 'I believe women can have it all, but a supportive employer is necessary', which was featured in 'The Women's Agenda'. I wanted to encourage others to 'say yes' and reassure them that if they wanted to, they could also get their new adventure of having a child to fit around their career.

A few years later, my friend and colleague Fiona Byarugaba was casually chatting to me about an opportunity she had been presented with. She said, 'I didn't know what to do and then I thought, "What would Emma do?" She would say yes and figure it out later!' It was very odd for me to hear this; I didn't realise my words would have such a profound impact. I was also surprised she even doubted herself—she was more than capable and fabulous at her job. Fiona has gone from strength to strength over the years and is now the DEI Lead (Diversity, Equity and Inclusivity) at Thoughtworks Australia. I caught up with her to reflect on her journey and find out why she even listened to me in the first place. This is Fiona's story:

> I've been observing you over time, and have worked with you on a couple of campaigns. One of the things I've admired about you is your can-do attitude. You'll say, 'There are four talks I need to do in a span of four months', and I'm like, that's crazy! You just say, 'No, I just need to do this, this and this'. You always see an opportunity, you don't let anything negative deter you and you always look for ways to improve something so you can repackage it to add value.

> I was presented with the opportunity to work on the global Thoughtworks Tech Radar, which was a whole new level for me — global, with a very executive audience—there was Martin Fowler, Neil Ford, Rebecca Parsons, Evan Bottcher . . . the whole tech advisory board!

> I was thinking 'Oh my goodness, how am I going to do that?' It's highly technical, and although I wasn't required to contribute technical expertise or content to the whole process—it was more bringing everyone together—I had never done anything like it on that level, with teams in different time zones and working with lots of heads across the organisation who were each experts in their field. I felt somewhat intimidated. But when I was approached, I thought of you and just said yes. Saying yes is the start of a commitment because you have to honour your word.

> I was thinking, how does Emma do it? Typically, you're pretty much working on your own and sometimes you don't have the budget to do things, you don't have stakeholder buy-in all the way like you need, but you start the conversations anyway—you plan and you make the business case regardless. CXD is a good example. In my case, it was more convincing myself I could do the job, even though I didn't know if I could.

I asked if she thought she had Imposter Syndrome:

> Yes, definitely. Karen Dumville [Global Head of Marketing Operations at Thoughtworks], my boss, said, 'I can't think of anyone better for the job, this is exactly something I can see you doing', and Gayarthi Rao, who I was taking over from, said the same. So I just went into it with the view of, what's the worst that can happen? But why do we always assume the worst—why don't we ever assume the best will happen?

> I've seen you do so many different things—including while pregnant!—and I remember the women's leadership article you wrote; it was like nothing could stop you. You're always leading the way and shining a torch on what we do—speaking at conferences, writing articles, challenging people, encouraging people and offering mentorship. So I really had no excuse. I knew if I needed guidance along the way, I could just ask you—it was actually a big part of the reason I said yes, and I'm not just saying that.

Other female colleagues complain about not being seen, but they're not prepared to get out of their comfort zones, and it's frustrating. I'd been wanting to move away from events and try something different for ages, and I just thought, 'How are things going to change if I'm not willing to step up?'

When we're willing to just say yes and see what happens, it can open other doors for us. But until we're brave enough to say yes, we'll never know. Fiona shared what doors have opened for her as a result of saying yes to the Tech Radar:

It improved my relationships with people and gave me a much better insight into their roles, responsibilities and what they do. It helped me demystify these key figures who are very well-known inside and outside the company. In the past, I had presented and worked with these people individually; this time I was presenting to all of them together. I had to remind myself that while they were very experienced and skilled in their field, they don't have the skills I have. I also needed to remind myself that I had to take that to the table—make recommendations, give guidance and let them learn from me too, because they don't know all the functions like I do. That mentality kept me going, and the more you talk to people the more you learn.

It also increased my credibility on a global level. I now get lots of people reaching out to me and asking for my guidance or asking me if we'd like to experiment with something in Australia first, and if I'd run it based on the work I did for the Tech Radar. I've also been called into global calls on various things, which didn't happen before.

Saying yes gave Fiona exposure on a global level across the organisation, and she took her knowledge to the table; she owned the space in which she's accomplished. A few years later, saying yes and proving herself led to her current role as DEI Lead at Thoughtworks Australia. Now, because of Fiona's position, she can see people's careers from a distance, which gives her good insights into what they struggle with:

It's not just your skills, it's how you communicate, collaborate and improve your relationships. Women who are aiming for leadership positions have a tougher time owning that. A man will say, 'I've worked in this role for this amount of time, I don't see why I can't get it', whereas women doubt themselves and often want to cross every 't' and dot every 'i'. Women have a better understanding of what's at stake and their accountability. And because there are fewer women in leadership roles, they have a heavier responsibility and need to prove themselves, whereas men don't have that same pressure, simply because there are more of them.

Sometimes saying yes then figuring it out is the same as you would do for any design challenge. If you love challenges and always try your best, how wrong can it really go? Failing isn't going to be the end of the world; no one is going to die, and if you manage stakeholders, articulate your progress and call out the risks, you can fall back on those, knowing you did all you could.

Cassandra observes:

> There are perfectionists everywhere in our design community; you have to learn to let go of that perfection. It doesn't mean not being close to the detail; it doesn't mean giving up on quality or standards. But actually, you know, you really have to learn to prioritise and pick your battles around what things are really important from a value perspective.

Women doubt themselves too much and are worried about putting themselves and their views out into the world for fear of failing or 'getting found out'. We put extra pressure on ourselves to be the best because we feel we're under greater scrutiny when we get things wrong, so we want to ensure we're 100% confident we're going to get it right before we say yes, especially when we're the minority or surrounded by more vocal people.

Quite simply, if we want to have more female role models, women need to start saying yes more and become the role models they wish they'd had. Embrace the same ambiguity we face when starting a design discovery, say yes and then figure out a way to solve the challenge.

We all need someone to aspire to

The need for and the importance of female role models isn't just an ideology; it's backed by multiple studies. Research by Pamela Sadler, Penelope Lockwood, Karen Fyman and Sarah Tuck[*] shows that female role models are key to inspiring other women to excel in areas where they may be under-represented. An article by Dr Margie Warrell, a bestselling author, leadership advisor and international authority on human potential featured in *Forbes,* talks about how 'female role models inspire girls to think bigger'.[†] She also found during her research that female leaders cited the positive impact of having strong female role models succeeding on their terms: 'Women demonstrated the ability to manage the responsibilities of career and family with authenticity and without apology'.

> ### Young women need female role models to inspire success.
>
> Helen Fraser, former Managing
> Director of Penguin UK

Having a role model helps us see what is possible and enables us to see and think differently, and this applies to all genders. However, we need to go beyond this; we

---

[*] Sadler, P., Lockwood, P., Fyman, K., Tuck, S. (2005). To Do or Not to Do: Using Positive and Negative Role Models to Harness Motivation. https://guilfordjournals.com/doi/10.1521/soco.22.4.422.38297

[†] Warrell, M. (2020). Seeing Is Believing: Female Role Models Inspire Girls To Think Bigger. Forbes.

need to be willing to support other women, not stand on them; and men and women need to support one another, not pull them down. One of my old clients and mentors, Steve Bolton, always talked about creating a circle of like-minded people around you and 'standing on the shoulders of giants', which may sound like a cliché but is relevant to creating 'allyship'. This is particularly crucial in the commercial world, consulting industry and often male-dominated organisations.

It doesn't matter where you are on your journey; it's important to build a network of trusted people around you and mentors that inspire you. Kathleen Casford's story is similar to those of other designers, where she has taken 'an explore and see what happens' approach to her career. She studied graphic design then moved to Boeing, where she became a technical drawer working with engineers who were designing aircraft. She then went back to finish her studies before moving to Melbourne, and then back to Brisbane, where she proceeded to find her feet as a designer.

Eventually she went on to start her own company, By Ninja; however, she needed help. Before attending the very popular, and now somewhat of an institution, The Design Conference in Brisbane, Australia, she did as many other eager designers do—stalked the speakers through social media before attending. However, Kathleen had a different plan—she was looking for a mentor to help her with her business. Through her stalking, she created a list of five designers she felt could best help her, based on their backgrounds.

Catriona Burgess (Head of Frost Place, part of Frost*collective) gave a talk that was very inspiring to Kathleen. 'I liked everything she said during her talk at the conference; it just resonated so much with me. I looked up to her and everything she said. I thought, I just want to be around this person to learn'.

But during the conference, while Kathleen had lots of opportunities to approach Catriona, she didn't. Instead, after the conference, she sent Catriona a rather unusual email titled 'Catriona, will you be mine?' She hoped it would get Cat's attention, based on her humorous personality. 'I thought, she'll either say no or best case she'll say yes. What have I got to lose?' Cat very soon became Kathleen's mentor off the back of that email. Kathleen reflected, 'I was really scared to do it, but now it's made it easier to ask people for help. The more I ask for help, the more people are saying yes, and over time I've gotten more confident asking people'.

While Kathleen's story may initially seem like she's oozing in confidence, confidence is one of the main things she and Cat work on in their sessions. Cat will often set challenges, such as sending Kathleen to networking events on her own, where she has to speak to a certain number of new people to help her confidence and to be more comfortable around people she doesn't know. Through this mentoring, Kathleen has learnt a lot about her self-worth:

> I want to make people happy and would often end up doing a lot more work or work for free than what was agreed. Cat helped me realise that in doing this, I was

actually lowering the value of design—not just for myself, but for everyone in the industry. Having a mentor who is in the same industry to support me, someone I admire and who has worked their way through the industry in challenging times, someone who has been through what I've gone through, normalises the struggles and doubt—I've learnt a lot so far.

Kahtleen's email to Catriona:

I sat in the dark, and watched you from a distance (creepy much?). I was inspired, and I learnt a lot (I have so many notes!), but I have so much more to learn. I've been searching for quite some time now, to find the one. A mentor. Someone I can learn from, share with, bounce ideas off, and hopefully who I can also give back to in my own way. I think you may just be that someone. What you had to say struck a big ol' rockstar chord with me.

Now's the point that I should probably clarify. I saw you speak (twice) at the Design Conference in May (hopefully less creepy now?). What resonated with me most was your holistic approach to creative solutions. And the truths and persona behind the brands that you help build. It's so much more than a logo, it's about generating authentic, life enriching design, that's backed by research.

Hi, my name is Kathleen, and I'm a creative problem solver.

I have a background in technical illustration and graphic design. Somewhere along the way I had a quarter-life-crisis and decided I wanted to be a mechanical engineer . . . yep . . . Anyway, long story short, I quit full time work in an agency in 2016 to finish my degree and accidentally started my own business (whoops). While it was a dream many years ago, it just took a really expensive degree in a completely unrelated field to get me there. The past two and a bit years have been an epic rollercoaster, and now I'm more excited about design than I ever have been. I really want to make something of this! That's where you come in. I really think you, and your journey, can help me grow into the designer I want to be.

I know mentoring isn't without its challenges—for starters, we're separated by approximately 730 kilometers of mostly barren land—but I hope you'll think I'm worth it. Plus, you know what they say about distance . . .

So, Catriona, will you be my mentor?

Kathleen Casford
Creative Overlord, By Ninja

"We all need to stay true to who we are and bring that to the table."

Don't become the worst version of yourself

Particular traits displayed by some male leaders, even some celebrated narcissistic characteristics, often result in women believing they have to display similar traits in order to break through the glass ceiling. This is exacerbated by those within the circle of influence advising and encouraging those who are trying to progress to adopt what are seen as more 'traditional' leadership traits. That's despite many stereotypical traits of male leaders' being the worst leadership traits, and women naturally having higher emotional intelligence.

As a result of this kind of expectation, we sometimes see women changing into the worst version of themselves. We can all tweak how we learn from situations to help us improve; however, changing into someone we are not and portraying traits that are unnatural to us can be hard work, and you may not like the person you become. While it's more common for women to encounter this, it's not limited to women.

Coming from large corporations like Fjord and Accenture® (with 540,000 people), Andy Polaine has experienced the 'boys' club' and seen how this mentality can turn some women into the opposite of what they really are in order to progress:

> Getting into leadership in the first place can be a boys' club—it's certainly a club. There's definitely a sense—and it's ridiculous—that it's much less to do with how good you are at something and much more to do with the sort of

allies and champions that you've buttered up along the way. There are a couple of things that feed into that. One is, you have traditionally got people who look like me—middle class, middle-aged white men—who are a certain type where, even in a group of fairly conscious people, there is a bit of a vibe of, 'Is this person one of us? Do we want to let them into the club of executive leadership?'

What I've seen a lot in corporate spaces is women who feel they have to become almost worse versions of terrible male leaders in order to push their way through into that environment. They have to be harsher; I don't want to say aggressive, because some men would see that as a positive thing—that it drives change—but I've definitely seen this type of bad behaviour on both sides of the gender divide.

Any discriminated-against group of people have to shout louder to get heard, and this creates a challenge for women. It goes back to a lot of socialisations in early life: 'Be quiet, do what you're told, don't rock the boat, be a good girl'. All those kinds of messages, in the playground, where boys get to scrabble around in sandpits, top to toe filthy, and it's fine, whereas if a girl gets all dirty, it's, 'Look what you've done to your dress!' All those really small things mount up.

Cassandra has also observed how some of the female leaders she knows have become more direct and sterner since joining leadership teams. Before the latest acquisition, the leadership team was still very much the design and tech leaders, and they had created a very relaxed and open environment where it was safe to call out bad behaviour in a tongue-and-cheek way; now it's a more corporate environment, with some leaders coming from a business consulting background, which brings a different vibe, not as relaxed as before.

Many of us, like Andy and Cassandra, have observed how some women are seen as less likeable once they adopt different traits in the belief it will help them get ahead. Research supports this observation and shows that women who are seen as successful and accomplished are also seen as aggressive and less likeable—labels not often applied to men in equal positions. Psychologists Madeline Heilman at NYU, Susan Fiske at Princeton, Laurie Rudman at Rutgers, Peter Glick at Lawrence, and Amy Cuddy at Harvard have repeatedly found that women face distinct social penalties for doing the very things that lead to success.

Marianne Cooper was the lead researcher for Sheryl Sandberg's *Lean In: Women, Work, and the Will to Lead*[*] and is a senior research scholar at the VMware Women's Leadership Innovation Lab at Stanford University. She has also proven through her research that women face social penalties for adopting certain behaviours that lead to success.

This conclusion is all too familiar to the many women on the receiving end of these penalties—the ones who are applauded for delivering results at work but then reprimanded for being 'too aggressive', 'out for herself', 'difficult', and 'abrasive'.

---

[*] Sandberg, S. (2013). *Lean In: Women, Work, and the Will to Lead*. Knopf. ISBN-13:978-0385349949

Just look at Jill Abramson, the first woman executive editor of *The New York Times,* who was described by staffers as 'impossible to work with' and 'not approachable' in a Politico article just days after *The Times* won four Pulitzer prizes (the third highest number ever received by the newspaper). The psychological research on success–likability penalties tells us that women and men can be viewed as similarly competent, yet still receive different likability scores. Scientific research also tells us that male and female leaders are liked equally when behaving participatively (i.e., including subordinates in decision-making), but when acting authoritatively, women leaders are disliked much more than men.

To be clear, it is not that women are always disliked more than men when they are successful, but that they are often penalised when they behave in ways that violate gender stereotypes. Being aware of this is important to truly evaluate what is really happening in companies and organisations like The New York Times. What is really going on, as peer-reviewed studies continually find, is that high-achieving women experience social backlash because of their very success—and specifically the behaviours that created that success—violates our expectations about how women are supposed to behave.

Women are expected to be nice, warm, friendly, and nurturing. Thus, if a woman acts assertive or competitive, if she pushes her team to perform, if she exhibits decisive and forceful leadership, she is deviating from the social script that dictates how she 'should' behave. By violating beliefs about what women are like, successful women elicit pushback from others for being insufficiently feminine or too masculine. As descriptions like 'Ice Queen' and 'Ballbuster' can attest, we are deeply uncomfortable with powerful women. In fact, we often don't really like them.

At the Women in Design 2017: Women Working Together event,* Laura Naylor; Bo Lu, Product Design Lead at Pinterest®; and Jamie Myrold, Senior Director of Experience Design at Adobe® openly shared some of the feedback they have received throughout their careers. It was suggested to Laura that she put more smiley faces in her emails because she appeared too aggressive. Bo Lu has been on teams where it's normal to talk over one another to get yourself heard, whereas her natural style is to wait until someone has finished before she gives her views, making her seem less dominant.

I can't please everybody, so I might as well be me.

Bo Lu, Product Design Lead at Pinterest

She divulged, 'I got feedback to be more assertive and visible. I tried it and got feedback that I was too aggressive and asked too many questions. I can't please everybody, so I might as well be me'. Jamie's views echoed those of Bo Lu: 'I've gotten feedback that I should be more assertive in meetings and speak louder, but it's just not my style. I

---

* https://www.designerfund.com/blog/women-design-2017-women-working-together

take the feedback and stay aware of my presence in executive-level meetings. But I'm not going to fake it just because someone says to be more assertive'. While some of these women have tried different styles, reverting back to their natural, less assertive nature hasn't prevented them from breaking through the glass ceiling in their design careers.

> **Learn to be more vocal in meetings or more confident talking about salary. Only seven percent of women negotiate their first salary, compared to fifty-seven percent of men.**
>
> Kim Mackenzie-Doyle

While we can all learn new things, improve who we are and become better at leading meetings, trying to fit into a box that isn't who we are is emotionally draining, and others can see when we're not comfortable. If we all try to act in a particular way, what example are we setting to others, and how can we progress towards a more acceptable work environment?

Cathy Lo is a Product Designer at Facebook® (now Meta). Her old boss, Maria Guidice, CEO of Hot Studio®, taught her the power of individuality. 'She would always be herself. What I've learnt from Maria and other mentors, like Facebook's VP of Design, Margaret Stewart, is that the key to success is to be yourself and don't be afraid'.

We need to stay true to who we are and bring that to the table. We also need to know our boundaries, what we are willing

What can you bring to the workplace that would give you the power to be the fierce leader you need to be?

to negotiate and not negotiate. Jamie Myrold recommends making a list of your core values to know what you really value in your life. 'What can you bring to the workplace that would give you the power to be the fierce leader you need to be?'

Inherent attitudes from the past are still impacting behaviour within the workplace, causing some women to feel like they need to behave differently or be labelled in a negative way. Organisations and individuals need to stop praising these attitudes and ensure that those we mentor—no matter if they're male or female—don't become the worst version of themselves or suffer from the likeability penalty. It's important that we all call out bad behaviour and support our peers. Let's hope we encounter fewer people who assume we're there to take the minutes.

Giving space and taking space

When designers join the tech world, they will find themselves in the minority because there is generally one designer to 10 developers, according to the Nielsen Norman Group's 2020 report, 'Typical Designer-to-Developer and Researcher-to-Designer Ratios' (see Figure 5.2). Then, because you are joining a statistically male-dominated industry, design leaders in the tech world have even more stacked against them.

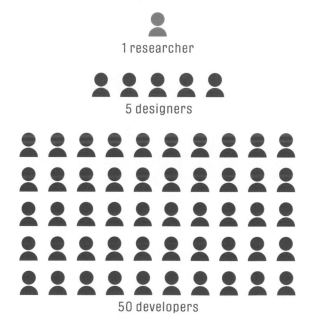

1 researcher

5 designers

50 developers

Figure 5.2   The most typical researcher-to-designer
-to-developer ratio reported in the survey was 1:5:50.*

---

*   Adapted from Kate Kaplan, 2010, Typical Designer-to-Developer and Researcher-to-Designer
    Ratios, Nielsen Norman, https://www.nngroup.com/articles/ux-developer-ratio/

These organisations already have very few women in leadership positions and even fewer in design leadership positions, making it harder for other designers to find inspirational leaders and see what is possible for them.

As designers, we know that diversity is critical to the success of products and experiences because it enables companies to create better and safer products that consider everyone, rather than one section of society. A report from McKinsey, 'Women in the Workplace 2021', found that diverse companies perform better, hire better talent, have more engaged employees, and retain workers longer than companies that do not. Data from the National Center for Women & Information Technology® (NCWIT) shows that of the 25% of women working in tech, the diversity within this group is further under-represented, with just 5% of the 25% being Asian women, while Black and Hispanic women accounted for 3% and 1%, respectively.

What small things can everyone do to help smooth out diversity and make the tech companies and consultancies more welcoming and inclusive? When I interviewed Erica Rider (DesignOps Leader at PayPal®, a very tech-heavy company), she was able to give an interesting perspective to this question.

Erica has a unique insight into what it's like being a designer in both a man's and a woman's world. Erica has two children and spent the first 50 years of her life as Eric. Not only did she spend most of her life as a white male designer seeing how other men acted and treated women, she also spent most of that time being conflicted by her gender. She said that transitioning has enabled her to feel more natural and herself. We laughed about how she thought she could get away with not telling anyone at work, especially as most of her time was spent on Zoom® during the COVID lockdown when everyone worked from home—who's going to notice that she suddenly looks different, and oh, she is now called Erica and not Eric? While Erica can bring two perspectives, she often gets Imposter Syndrome.

> I get asked to do things like being part of 'women in tech' groups. I know I spent most of my life passing as a white man, and with that came privileges, and I learnt things from those privileges that a woman, trans woman or cis woman would never have experienced, or that they would have experienced differently to me and that I didn't have to go through. What I struggle with is that the women's communities are so welcoming to me, and I feel guilty because I didn't go through what they went through.

What can we all learn from Erica?

She observed that being nurturing and having empathy comes more naturally to women, which reflects what I mentioned earlier. But Erica has also seen how women want to be taken seriously and feel they have to act in a particular way—they want a seat at the table but are unsure if they should take it. As far as she's concerned, 'If you walk into a room and no one is sitting there, just sit there. If you want a seat at the table, take it'.

Erica has also observed that men tend to talk over one another, whereas women don't, and there have been numerous studies that support this. The way we interact and communicate will also differ from social settings to the workplace. World-renowned gender communication expert Deborah Tannen believes that men speak to determine and achieve power and status, whereas women talk to determine and achieve connection. This observation supports women's naturally higher emotional intelligence.

Don Zimmerman and Candace West are sociologists at the University of California–Santa Barbara. In their study, 'Sex Roles, Interruptions and Silences in Conversations', they found that, 'There are definite and patterned ways in which the power and dominance enjoyed by men in other contexts are exercised in their conversational interaction with women'. The study analysed 31 two-party conversations recorded in public places, such as cafés, convenience stores, and university campuses. Of the 31 conversations, 10 were between two men, 10 between two women, and 11 between a man and a woman. In the two same-sex groups combined, the authors found seven instances of interruption. In the mixed group they found 48 interruptions, 46 of which were instances where a male had interrupted the female.

Erica tries to instil a different way of thinking into the younger people she coaches to allow women the chance to be heard:

> Have you seen men talk over each other? If you want to talk amongst a group of men, you just start talking, even if others are already talking—you just talk until the other person stops. Women don't tend to do that; they give space for other women to talk. When you have men and women together, men tend to take advantage of this and often don't give the space to allow women to talk—this is something I now make a conscious effort to do.

Erica is now trying to instil this idea of being more conscious about giving space in the younger generation. She coaches kids' roller derby and tries to educate the boys about giving the space to allow the girls to talk, while encouraging the girls to take the space. 'It's your space, you don't ask for permission'.

While we need to be more conscious about giving everyone space to share their opinions, we also need to consider cultural differences and language patterns. A friend of mine was in a meeting during which a male colleague of a similar senior position was talking through something, and she was trying to interject at what she saw as natural pauses and opportunities for her to ask questions and add to the conversation. Later, he pulled her to one side and highlighted that he thought she was rude for trying to interrupt.

When she told me what had happened, and knowing both of them, I explained the theory of speech patterns and rhythms and suggested that maybe it was to do with cultural differences. English isn't his first language, and from what I had observed from working with him, he likes to think things through as he's talking and takes long pauses as he's explaining an idea, so maybe what she took as a pause or space wasn't that to him.

These days, with many meetings being held over Zoom, Microsoft® Teams® or Google® Meet®, we have the added complexity of either not noticing indicators in body language that someone wants to speak or 'false spaces' due to internet lag. Sometimes, by the time a space is created, the conversation has moved on, and the point someone wanted to make is no longer relevant or ends up taking the conversation back a few steps.

We need to remember we're just human, and with every mistake or success we learn. Anyone who has the persistence to keep forging ahead is going to succeed, and if you don't get the support you need, don't be afraid to take your energy somewhere that appreciates you and will give you the space to be heard and succeed.

While it's going to take time to improve the gender imbalance within tech, if we can all make a simple effort to give people the space they need and ensure everyone is heard, we can enable those who are under-represented to have a voice.

Where there's a problem, find solutions

As discussed in Chapter 1, when presenting a problem to a client, it's important not to just hand over the problem and leave it to them to find a solution. Use your design skills to explore the problem and present it together with possible solutions. This will give you more credibility, demonstrate leadership and turn it into a discussion where you are with them in forming the best way forward. Use your design skills to your advantage, consider who you are presenting the problem to and think about it from the perspective of the business.

The same is true for your career. If you want to head in a certain direction, you want to achieve something in particular or you've encountered a problem, rather than presenting the challenge for your employer to solve, instead go in with, 'This situation has come up, and these are some possible solutions to resolve the issue', or 'I just wanted to bring it to your attention to keep you in the loop, but I've already got a plan in place'. It might even be, 'I want to achieve this, and here's some of the support I think I will need, which I'd like to discuss'. Demonstrating you've put some thought into the problem or goal will elicit a more positive response and open the discussion.

For example, when I was discussing the time I would need to write this book, I spoke about how my book aligned with one of our strategic goals, and because I had written a book before, I knew what it entailed. I believed I could balance time for billable and non-billable work and gave examples of how that would work with the project I was on at the time. I also presented how I could still achieve results for clients, not be too much of a cost to the business and how the business would benefit from it.

But I've noticed that many of the women I have mentored, especially on the leadership programme, don't feel they deserve to ask for what they want. That's crazy to me! If the company didn't feel they were deserving, they wouldn't have selected them to be on a leadership programme or put them forward for a promotion. As my mum always says to me, 'If you don't ask, you don't get', and as Kathleen shared, the more she asked for help, the more help she got and the easier it became to ask.

Another observation is that women also tend to focus on all the reasons why they *can't* do something instead of thinking about how they *can* do something, or they find it hard to take a step back to think about the problem differently and develop other options. For instance, they might want to share something they have learnt to help others, but they're not confident speaking in public. If that's you, think about how you could deliver your message differently, maybe through a talk to a smaller group, a blog or even pairing with someone who is a seasoned speaker.

I've also seen designers—both male and female—who assume their opinions aren't valid simply because they are the minority on delivery teams. They focus on their position in the team, rather than realising they are there to ensure the team solves the problem—and solves it from a human perspective. Even if you're not confident enough to voice your opinion among the entire team, seek out allies; or as Andy mentioned, if the majority of the team is male and you're female, find a male advocate who will support you and your opinions. This will help amplify your message and help get buy-in.

Whatever situation you're in, give yourself space to see the problem or goal you want to achieve from a distance, and think about different ways to solve it. Seek the help of others to support you and get team members to echo what you're saying. You don't have to be the loudest person in the room; there are other ways to get your voice heard. A client of mine would often say 'Emma, we have a problem—no, I mean we have a challenge'. Something as simple as replacing the word 'problem' with 'challenge' can really help change your mindset. However you do it, don't let any inner anxious or hesitant voice take over and prevent you from progressing to be the best version of yourself. You're where you are because you deserve to be there, and you have just as much right to achieve your goals and aspirations as anyone else.

Organisations will only change if we make them change

People and organisations don't set out to make things difficult; often they are not aware there is a problem, so it's our responsibility to raise awareness by bringing attention to inequality and bad behaviour when we see it. Ian Kelsall believes that building a culture where certain traits will not be tolerated by team members or the organisation, no matter your position, goes a long way towards building high-performing and diversified teams.

> Thoughtworks typically attracts and hires people with a greater sense of empathy and self-awareness and therefore probably indexes much higher on imposter syndrome because of this. I have observed that, as a community, our designers

who identify as male wouldn't necessarily conform to the stereotypical male designers who push or exaggerate their expertise to attain leadership positions. I don't think anyone who would attempt to do that would be tolerated for long.

Building a culture where it's safe to call out bad behaviour and knowing what hills you're willing to die on will, over time, help the organisation change. It could be small changes—for instance, your team or usability testing participants lack adequate diversity for the product or service you're building—call it out, don't wait for someone else to say it. Equally, you don't want to be the person who points it out all the time, so it's about educating others to recognise it.

If you feel your career isn't going in the direction you want, speak up. People are not mind readers—if you don't make it known what you want to do, how can they know that a change needs to be made? The road won't always be smooth, and if they say no without good reason, then find somewhere else or someone who will back you. As one of the directors at a Big 4 consulting firm noted earlier, 'Anyone who can take a bit of pushback and keep going is going to succeed'.

When I spoke to a female designer at one of the large consulting firms, she told me she had been knocked back on a promotion due to some feedback. 'When they gave me the feedback, I was so upset and confused, it just didn't make sense—it was completely different to the feedback I'd been gathering and the opposite of everything I had been doing over the last few years'. After she confided in other close female leaders, they were equally as confused:

> It was great to offload to them, I knew they would be honest with me, which is what I wanted. They recommended three things: One was to speak to other more influential leaders in the company who knew me and whom I could trust to give an honest opinion. I then needed to take all the evidence I had and present it in a business case style, a bit similar to how we present our customer research findings. Then I needed to approach the person making the decision. But, instead of just saying I don't agree with the decision, my friend said I should take a Sheryl Sandberg approach and ask for help.

For those of you who are not familiar with one of Sheryl's approaches, it's to present things in a way that you are asking for help. Why? Because people like to help.

> I contacted a few influential people I could trust and asked for their help. They were shocked by the feedback, which was reassuring; they also offered to help further and gave me their own feedback, which I added to my business case. It was a lot of work, but everyone was very supportive and that spurred me on.

> I wrote an email to one of the main people involved in the original decision, explaining the situation in a logical manner and asking for help. It worked! She was very keen to help me understand the discrepancy and give me more constructive feedback, then she ended up doing an investigation, which was amazing—I

really didn't expect it to be taken so seriously. It transpired that the feedback through the process had been the same positive feedback I'd collected—but all the positive feedback had been misread as negative! I couldn't believe it! How could it be misinterpreted, and who else had this happened to?

Shortly thereafter, she went on to get the promotion, but would that have happened if she hadn't spoken up and continued to push ahead? This story shows how important it is to raise issues when they happen, gain support from those around you and have strong leaders who inspire you and have your back. If something isn't right, be comfortable speaking up. That could be with your own career, how someone treats you or how someone else is being treated. People and organisations can only solve problems that they know exist.

> **"McKinsey estimated that gender parity would add 12 trillion dollars to the global economy by 2025."**

So, in summary . . .

Changing systemic attitudes that have been passed down through generations takes time, and organisations will only become more diversified, with more female leaders, if more people give women and other minority voices space—and they themselves develop the confidence to say 'yes', even if they haven't got things 100% figured out. There is insurmountable evidence to show that more diversified teams lead to better products, better experiences and often more successfully run organisations.

While the COVID-19 pandemic has had a huge impact on some women and added to their responsibilities, research shows it has shone a light on the strengths we bring to leadership tables, strengthening the argument that gender diversity within teams and at the decision-making level leads to better outcomes for all stakeholders. McKinsey estimated that gender parity would add 12 trillion dollars to the global economy by 2025, which reinforces the case to push harder for more opportunities for women to become leaders.

If we want the industry and design careers to change for the better, yes, we need organisations to change, but more women need to be brave and forge ahead through the bumps, bringing other women along with them. We also need to ensure that it's not only women mentoring women—mentors should be diverse, and we should all be helping one another and learning together. Strong men, even if they're not in leadership roles themselves, can be some of the best advocates for women, and what's most important is that you have an encouraging mentor who supports you and understands where you're headed, regardless of their gender. My most inspirational mentors have all been male.

Policies around more flexible working schedules and support for parents need to improve, which can be a stretch for some smaller organisations that simply can't offer the same as large consultancies—and nor should they be expected to. But being more flexible in when and where you work, especially as a designer in today's tech world, should be easily achievable, and COVID has helped change that mindset.

Throughout your journey you will undoubtedly face pushback, but how you handle it will help shape you. See pushback as a challenge: Why are they pushing back? What can you do to persuade them differently? Do they have a point that you should consider, and will addressing that make your argument stronger? Don't be defeated at the first hurdle; learn, adapt, say yes, and then figure it out later. And if you can't see your career going the way you want in your current organisation, find somewhere else where you can flourish.

And so important: don't fall into the bearpit where you become the worst version of yourself. You do not need to change who you are in order to get to the top. You may need to change how you approach things, be more succinct with your storytelling and hone your influencing and persuading techniques; but be confident in your execution and nurture those around you so that they can also achieve their full potential and become the best versions of themselves. Stay authentic and play nicely with other humans, otherwise the top can be lonely.

Always do what you're afraid to do.

Ralph Waldo Emerson

six

up your influence

Working in a design agency requires you to hone your craft and demonstrate you're a great designer, and you may have to convince clients why they should choose you over another agency, or why you feel your design is the right solution. But in a tech or business consultancy, it becomes infinitely more complex to show design's worth. So how can you influence in a world that isn't yours? Where do you find advocates inside client organisations to influence design's position and learn tips from design and tech leaders on how to influence in this space?

Some believe leadership is about dominance, charisma and a healthy dose of downright arrogance. As I discussed earlier, this may get some people to the top, but it won't gain you respect or win you many advocates along the way. To influence as a leader, you need to build followers, which requires understanding, listening, kindness, passion and a vision—if people believe in your vision, they will follow. As you develop a relationship with the people you inspire as followers, you also need to recognise and reward them so that they feel appreciated and heard.

Many people on delivery teams, especially if they are building a new product, just focus on getting the first release over the line within the allocated timescale. There may be pressure from above to meet deadlines in order to look good in an upcoming election, or for execs to receive bonuses, regardless of whether the product is human-centred or a success when launched. But when it's not a success and customer complaints come in, it won't be those getting the bonuses on the receiving end, it will be the teams who have worked hard to build the product and whose voices went unheard when raising issues. You need to make your stakeholders look good and they need to trust and believe you will.

So you need to appreciate that often there is more at play—considerations and motivations beyond the project itself—which is why you as a design leader need to develop a deeper knowledge and understanding of how the organisation operates. You've got to know who you need to influence to get concerns and risks raised early, find out what your stakeholders biggest fears are, and how can you use this information to frame your case in a way that enables you to ensure the best possible experience is created, especially when it's the first release.

Throughout my career, I have witnessed people who can't actually do the thing they're meant to be doing rise up through the ranks simply because they have a 'silver tongue'—leaving me scratching my head as to how they've actually managed it! Andy Polaine's experience is that, 'What you say and not what you actually do will get you into leadership—sometimes just the right words are enough to get you the ears of people to get things done'. But not all of us find it easy to construct intelligent, well-thought-out ideas and arguments. A large part of influencing and being a DesignedUp leader is about empathy and understanding what is really going on.

Andy has spent a number of years observing what drives many of the execs that we as design leaders have to influence:

> A large part of it is really about the underlying thing. Operating as a leader is understanding the fear and anxiety, and men are much, much more fearful than

I think people believe. It's weird, middle-aged men are in a position of privilege, right? They are the dominant, privileged group, and yet they're all completely riddled with fear and anxiety.

You need to understand what triggers their behaviour—how do you unlock what is really going on and understand why someone might react in a certain way? Usually it's because they're afraid of something. You need to establish what it is they're afraid of and decide how you can present what you're trying to do to achieve the goal and eliminate their fear. That's an important skill. You need the ability to understand and tune into their fears and concerns and talk with confidence.

We had been bought in to rescue a project that had hemorrhaged millions from a lack of leadership and a team that didn't know what being a team meant. We had to prove ourselves quickly to the client and demonstrate that we could do what we had promised. That meant influencing inside the organisation so we could grow our reputation and demonstrate we could turn their situation around—show them how we'd made improvements and advances with the product and team within a short period of time.

It became apparent early on that the organisation used a lot of internal PR to advocate for the work they were doing, which required regular board meetings and organisation-wide presentations to showcase the progress of projects, all of which would help towards securing further funding. Some of this internal PR involved creating videos to showcase the work, which some saw as a waste of money and time, especially those who didn't understand the power of internal PR. Compelling videos help tell the story and show how real people are doing the work, and they're usually far more engaging than a presentation—you can actually watch the teams working and see virtually first-hand how they have solved the problems.

This project was a huge mission, with daily discoveries of technical and user experience problems, not to mention outdated ways of working and lack of skills in some of the original team members. The execs didn't always understand the technical constraints, but I knew they were keen on human-centred design. Although I wasn't convinced they really knew what it meant, I did know it was an important tick box for them, and over time I could educate them about what being human-centred meant and the value and importance of creating a great user experience.

The project had a lot of eyes on it. The programme manager had our many workshops filmed to help her promote the project we were rescuing and how we were doing it. It was the exemplar project that would lead the way in agile design and delivery, so it needed to clearly demonstrate to other teams and the organisation how products should be created.

We invited a wide group of people across the organisation to our showcases, which we ran at the end of every iteration (every two weeks). While explaining all the issues we'd uncovered may have seemed like a good idea, I was conscious that it would only have reminded them how badly the project was failing prior to the rescue. You don't want to rub salt in the wounds in these situations—they just need to know everything is being fixed and they're going to get a great result at the end after spending millions of dollars.

"Ninety percent of everything that comes to our mind is by visual stimuli.*"

Understanding what was important to them and what their fears were enabled us to ensure we told a story that resonated. Knowing the audience would have different levels of knowledge of tech, design and continuous delivery, we ensured we kept the information at a level everyone could understand and weaved in user stories to help demonstrate our progress.

During an iteration, I discovered a user-experience problem that had been created by the previous team. After we had tested a few different options that were technically feasible and solved the problem with users, I saw an opportunity to show visually how much we'd changed the product since joining. While we could have gone with a basic-looking UI, I knew going the extra mile and adding the polish would add more impact that the execs and users would quickly notice and would enhance the experience. I also knew from previous experience that the extra polish was really easy to implement from a tech perspective.

However, I also knew the UI change would get pushback from our tech lead.

* https://www.researchgate.net/publication/220208334_Attention_web_designers_You_have_50_milliseconds_to_make_a_good_first_impression_Behaviour_and_Information_Technology_252_115-126

Fortunately, I had a good relationship with him and knew he would be reasonable if the idea was presented in the right way. So, when the expected pushback came, I explained that I understood his concern. I showed empathy and understanding and reassured him that I was listening. I explained that in any other circumstance I would absolutely agree that the extra polish to enhance the experience could be left until a little later; but in this case, we needed to show an immediate impact to a very visual client, and this was a 'quick win' in return for the effort. If we could make the change, not only did it highlight the user problem we had solved, but the extra visual impact would be something they would walk away remembering.

He understood that it was more for some positive PR around the project, and we worked together on how best to make it simple to implement, while still creating the impact. Explaining a valid reason for the request had removed any assumption I was just being a 'difficult designer', and by using my influence and working together, the required outcome was achieved.

The change had a profound impact: the product owner was re-ignited with excitement when I showed him what we wanted to do, other teams started talking positivly about the project and the great work was relayed to the board. This wasn't just because of the visual work; it was all the effort the entire team had put into turning things around, and it gave us the PR story and immediate impact we needed. The entire team was now rejuvenated and excited to work on a sexy-looking product.

Many people underestimate the impact great visuals have on us human beings, yet 90% of everything that enters our mind is via visual stimuli. And, as I've already mentioned, you have just 50 milliseconds before users have made their first judgements on a digital product.

Influencing people you don't already have a relationship with

Sometimes we may need to influence people we don't have an existing relationship with, and I treat these situations as I would any sales pitch. If you're familiar with design agency pitches, it's about telling the story, setting the vision, the problem you're trying to solve and how you're going to solve it. Sometimes you might need to swap 'this is how you're going to solve the problem' for a presentation of different options, so you can let people share their ideas and come to a consensus. This approach allows everyone to feel happy and part of the decision, and it gives everyone a chance to voice their opinion.

So how does this work in practice? During the COVID-19 crisis, I was working remotely, like the majority of people in the world. I needed to get two departments with employees who had been capturing and analysing their data in two different ways for over 20 years to agree on a new method for completing this critical element of their jobs. Prior to the crisis, I'd only had a face-to-face relationship with two of them, and the remaining people I'd only 'met' through online usability testing. As well as getting them to agree on a new approach, I had to influence them to choose the easier option to build, while ensuring it was still intuitive for the employees of both departments and solved the problem.

We had a tight budget, and they had no idea how much it cost to develop platforms, having little or no knowledge about how systems are designed and built. The decision they were going to make would dramatically affect the way they worked and would either result in our being able to build the platform within budget or require sacrificing other features, which would drastically affect the possibility of getting further budget. The decision would also affect many other people.

I approached them with the message that we needed their help, making them feel valued and setting the tone that their opinions mattered. I then reminded them of the vision for the platform: 'Bringing two legacy systems together to prevent duplicate data and create a better way of working'.

I then went through the top employee pain points identified during interviews and research that they'd been involved with. I walked them through the problems we'd uncovered and some possible solutions, which we'd created as a team to ensure they solved the problem, were intuitive and were technically possible.

After presenting the options, I reminded them of the vision before asking for their opinions and whether they were happy to vote on which solution they preferred—or if they had a better option. Bringing the vision back in at the end reiterated what we were trying to achieve, and opening it up for discussion allowed them to have their say and be part of the solution.

This wasn't a highly polished presentation; it was simply sharing my screen with my design artboard, having a few key points with the vision and then the rough ideas. This implied it wasn't finalised and was open for change and their input.

We had an open and honest discussion, sharing thoughts and ideas, then we used the chat function in Microsoft® Teams® to vote on a decision. The majority voted the way we hoped they would. This decision was a huge step towards building the product vision and was something the business could use to present to the board. Being a design leader allows you to act as the glue between users, the business and development teams, and you can use your influence to drive the direction and vision for a product.

The users are happy because you've solved their problem, made their job easier and listened to them; the developers are happy because they were involved in the conversation and are on board with the tech solution; the business is happy because you're not blowing the budget; and the board and stakeholders who are ultimately paying for the product are happy because you're realising their vision, bringing it in on budget and ensuring it's solving the right problem.

It's not all on you though—it's a team sport. Remember that you're all in it together, and celebrating the wins and rewarding your team for their effort shows appreciation and helps teams bond. It can be something simple as buying their favourite brand of gourmet chocolate milk. As Mike Mason mentioned in Chapter 1, you need to ensure the reward is something decent that will be appreciated—don't just buy any superstore-brand donuts, buy the gourmet ones.

> ### There are two things people want more than sex and money—recognition and praise.
>
> Mary Kay Ash

Show them what's possible

When you're influencing, sometimes you have to show an idea and make it tangible in order for people to understand it—they need to see and feel what you're talking about. You'll find this a lot in tech consultancies because you'll often be working with clients and their customers who don't know what is possible; they'll default to what's familiar to them, which is no good if you're trying to break new ground or get them to think in terms of modern ways to design products.

But it can be hard to justify the time, money and effort involved in going out and creating something just to show the client and customers what you mean. One way to overcome this is to phrase it as a 'spike'—can we 'spike' this out or 'timebox' or 'create a quick-and-dirty prototype?' Using these words can help get it over the line, as they remove the assumption that they're going to have to spend money on something they don't understand.

Another way is to go 'rogue', which I love doing. If I know for sure something will work and that the best way to explain what I mean is by showing, I'll work on it in my spare time. Remember Grace Hopper's saying that it's easier to ask for forgiveness than for permission? Erica Rider is also a fan of showing what's possible and not asking for permission. She saw an opportunity to improve a process at PayPal®, where it would take them a day to create a mock-up in their current app. So she came up with an idea to speed up the process of prototyping and testing using UX Pin®. However, many people in the organisation didn't understand the concept and what it would do for them. She explained the idea to a team member, and without asking the engineer, he developed a solution over the weekend. Monday morning, he came to her and said 'What do you think of this? Look what I did'.

> Wow! I didn't think he was actually going to do something—he had built six components that were working. I showed my boss and he said, 'I now understand what you've been talking about for the last year. People just thought you were crazy but right now, seeing this, it all makes sense.' It finally clicked for him, and he funded us to do a proof of concept.

Erica and her team managed to reduce a process that used to take a day down to 10 minutes, eventually getting to the point where one member of her team could build a live prototype in a few minutes. To expand the use of the new product further, they looked at how it could speed up some of the work undertaken by product managers. Through understanding some of the problems product managers have, they were able to create a smooth transition between the tool they were currently using and their new tool, which enabled information to be rendered automatically, drastically speeding up their processes. The tool was further scaled to help the UX team improve processes between the 1 designer–311 developer ratio.

> We showed them what the new tool could do. They told us about other things they wanted to do, and we said, 'We can do that'. We showed we could build a live prototype in two minutes, fully functioning with working charts, detailed lists that filtered and sorted and a working navigation. Everything worked perfectly, and they could see me building it and how easy it was. That's when everything just switched. The CTO wanted stats to see how efficient our new tool was, so we ran some tests to compare the new tool and process with the existing one, and were able to show a dramatic improvement in efficiency.

There are many ways to up your influence and get yourself and your ideas noticed so you can make a difference. You don't need to be arrogant or narcissistic to achieve success; what you need is to have people who trust you and followers who support you—team members who will take your idea and build it without asking. You need to be empathetic and able to predict what the other person's response might be in advance by understanding their fears, anxieties and what drives them. Then you can be ready with the right answer or frame your approach in such a way that they won't be resistant to your idea.

Influencing successfully is not easy, and sometimes your approach won't work, or you've misunderstood who the person is or what they want to achieve, but if you don't try you will never know.

Mixing technology and design

To succeed and influence effectively inside a tech company or consultancy, design leaders need to pay attention to the business needs of both the consultancy and the client. You also need to understand technology (to a degree) and it's constraints and find your advocates from the tech side. You need to bring this all together for success. If you want to ensure your solution gets the business's approval and can be built, as a design leader, you need to understand not only the business goals but also the technical constraints. You'll need to find tech advocates who understand design and care about being human centred; you'll need to understand what tech stacks are being used and how this impacts design decisions or helps define the tech stack.

Design leaders need to balance the users' needs, the product vision and technology constraints (see Figure 6.1). Yes, you've got to push for great experiences and keep reminding the development team of the vision to prevent them from getting stuck on the now, but you also need to consider the tech constraints to ensure the vision can actually be met.

We were nearing completion of the first delivery phase of a new product and were in parallel discussions for planning the next phase and negotiating contracts. During a co-design session for an upcoming story card, we discovered that the managers, who would be using the feature for adding a user to a new project, could add the same person to the project multiple times due to tech constraints. Although the managers made up a small percentage of users, we didn't want to give them a bad experience, with a knock-on effect on users who had been added multiple times.

As a team, we discussed the best ways to overcome this small issue, and along with some of the managers who would be using the feature, agreed on a lightweight solution that balanced the user experience with technology and kept us on our delivery target. However, one person in the team, who was not a designer but a quality analyst, was pushing us to take it further and create an even better experience for the user. It would have been much more complicated to implement, and spending unnecessary time over-polishing this small item that would not add any value and could take away from the effort we had allocated for more important items that would really impact the users' workflow.

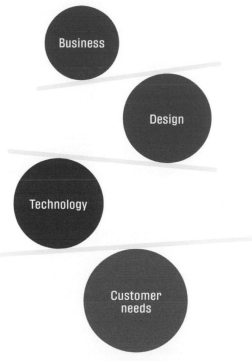

Figure 6.1 Balancing user needs, product vision and tech constraints

191

So I reminded the team that we had more important things to work on, that the solution we'd already agreed on solved the problem, and those who would be using it had also agreed on the solution. I also reminded them that once in use, if we received feedback that it wasn't clear enough, we could then improve it further.

As designers, it's easy for us to lose focus and become consumed with perfecting a solution—and even easier when a team member is pushing for polishing something. This is a time when you need to step up as a design leader, wear your business and tech hats to see the wider picture, then use your range of influencing skills to keep everyone on the team on track—ensuring we align with the tech leaders, who are also trying to meet the vision and keep the project on course.

Darren Smith, who started his career as a developer and worked his way up through the ranks to become Chief Product & Technology Officer at MYOB (one of the top cloud accounting products in Australia), says mixing technology and design and perfecting the solution is all about 'balance':

> I often ask myself, is it good enough, does it expose us to risk, is there time later to fix stuff? Slowing yourself down too much to get something perfect is not the right state, nor is going too fast, breaking things and not paying attention to the risks, so it is always about finding the right balance. You want a great product that gives people a nice experience, but then you also don't want to spend loads of time working on that because technology moves so fast and customers' expectations change a lot. It's about solving the actual problem while maintaining a balance between what's beneficial to the business and what's beneficial to the customer.

Not all technical leaders understand design, and this can be true both inside the consultancy and with the client. Tech leaders are not always that open to collaborating on solving a problem, and some are so focused on delivering a great technical solution that they forget about the people who will be using it. As a design leader it's your job to ensure the customer is at the centre of the process and to remind everyone on the team who the users are, what problems you're trying to solve and what the latest feedback has been. You may even encounter some tech leads who believe you can avoid usability testing to save time, and just rely on your years of design experience to make critical decisions that could impact a significantly large number of users—despite knowing very little about the user group and dealing with an organisation you have little context on, given that the project is still in its early days!

The reality is that usability testing isn't just about getting feedback from users to ensure you build the right thing and to help you understand the users better as a team. It's also about gathering data and insights to enable you to tell the story of the customer and why Approach A is better than Approach B. Sometimes you may have to use the data as part of your strategy to persuade product owners to think differently, especially when they are new to the role and only see the product as they would use it themselves, rather than from the perspective of how users out there actually want to use it. Design, whether in an agency or a consultancy, has always been about pitching the design idea and the rationale behind it, and how we can add to it with customer data, customer insights, technical constraints, solutions and business insights to create a compelling argument to persuade and influence.

From the various conversations I've had with designers and developers from across different tech consultancies and companies, I've learnt we're all trying to improve how product delivery works for digital products by unifying human-centred design, design thinking and traditional agile delivery. Some are further along on the journey than others, having made a conscious effort to significantly invest in improving and reinventing their product delivery capability. They are now making small advances in the way design and technology work together, or how to perfect agile ways of working to better incorporate user feedback, ensure we're not running too fast or too slow and have the time to ideate and test on users so we build the right thing.

Getting clients to where they need to be, especially if they are 10–15 years behind, is always going to be a challenge for both designers and delivery teams. The most common discussion we all seem to have, especially with clients, is around agility and being able to incorporate design and technology, working together as one cohesive team, ensuring we are always driving the right thing to market and making sure to start the conversation from the customer or employee mindset—what are their needs and how will this impact them?

Andreas Markdalen, Global Chief Creative Officer at frog®, feels the biggest conflict might be during the delivery phase, when tech people want to focus on reacting to current items that sit in the backlog rather than taking a customer mindset and looking at the bigger picture:

> There is always that gap between iterating on the status quo versus transforming a long-term vision. It's about identifying a vision that will make people excited—something aspirational to aim for—while not losing track of the current. When we start an engagement with a new client, there will almost always be a set backlog with priorities based on the tech stack or the available tech platforms. Sometimes the customer's voice has been lost in the mix; other times the trajectory just isn't bold enough. There's a disconnect with the overarching strategic vision or long-term product roadmap. We always try to bring the focus back to the long-term vision and adjust the backlog accordingly. It's hard to get that balance right, since you want to keep delivering through the transformation; alignment is needed from Day 1.

In situations like this, it's good to be able to fall back on the agreements made at the start of a project, where you look at the trade-off sliders, design principles or similar, and have the discussion around that initial agreement. What customer or user insights do we have and what are the tech constraints or other reasons for doing something one way over another? Bringing all that information together will help with prioritising where to focus and can also lead to a worthwhile discussion around whether the team is still happy with the agreed trade-off sliders and whether anything pertinent has changed in the business.

It always amuses me in workshops when execs prioritise UX over time and budget. From my experience, it rarely plays out like that. It's great that they want it to be that way, but more often than not, in the real world, it comes down to money and time. You still place the user at the centre, but you have to make trade-offs, first build the 'lite' version that meets their needs and gives a good experience, then place the enhancements that will turn it into an even better experience into the backlog, ready to be prioritised later.

These conversations rely on you as a design leader taking the client and the delivery team on the journey to thinking from a customer-centred point of view—and push your case for not prioritising things just because the exec or tech lead want it. This is where you need to use your story-telling skills to influence; bring all the data points together and show that you've listened to their point of view, you've understood the tech constraints—so how can we get what the customer wants to work within the parameters that we have? Collaborate with them to find a solution that takes all the points on board.

Andreas and I were discussing the balance of competing priorities and how we ensure the customer stays central to the conversation:

> It's not design versus tech, it's about finding a good balance. Initially we might pitch these really forward-looking concepts in an ideation or immersion phase that could portray a future state a few years ahead. A tech platform transformation might be necessary to get there. The question becomes, what are the trade-offs, and how can we move forward while meeting the expectations of the customer throughout the journey?

> I think it's really interesting that this idea of immersing yourself into the field, gathering insights from people in a qualitative or quantitative fashion, still feels kind of radical, even though it's such a well-documented and well-defined process now; and I think everyone has been talking about human-centred design or design thinking. But still, you come into the conversations with different companies, and it's not the norm, it still feels provocative. It's been surprising to me over the last few years that we're still selling that as 'emerging innovation', where it should be established at this point.

Now that more and more tech companies, consultancies and organisations are embracing design and becoming more customer and digital focused, we need to remember that many of these organisations were first and foremost driven by either technology or business, and the very foundations they were built on do not easily flex—especially those with legacy tech, data that's not clean or in human language, design and customer insight silos and a waterfall approach to building solutions.

They can't pivot quickly to embrace customer insights and embed design into their delivery needs, which was one of the drivers behind creating the design thinking methodology; it was a way of explaining how we work to people who thought we were whimsical creatives who lived in an unrealistic world of the future.

Nevertheless, technology companies that adopt an agile approach really should have no excuse not to be customer and consumer (or user) focused, especially when two of the 12 principles behind the Agile Manifesto are:

1. Our highest priority is to satisfy the customer through early and continuous delivery of valuable software.
2. Welcome changing requirements, even late in development. Agile processes harness change for the customer's competitive advantage.*

Some may argue that the Manifesto focuses only on the end customer and not on employees and other users of software and digital products. Everyone needs to be viewed and treated as the 'customer', everyone wants a good experience, even if they are not directly paying for the product or service.

In theory, agile principles should help ensure technology is approached with a human-centered mindset, but not everyone follows the principles. Rebecca Parsons of Thoughtworks says that when joining a tech consultancy or working with their clients who might be tech focused, we need to remember that the tech culture is the dominant culture.

> You're kind of in their house, so the onus falls a little bit on the designers to try to bridge that communication gap. We speak different languages, and, most dangerously, there might be words that you use as a designer that mean one thing to you and something very different to a tech exec—and that's when conversations can really go wrong.

> So, the first thing to do as a designer is try to figure out how you can translate your worldview—your principles—into a language that's understandable to a technologist. You already have all of the tools to help you get into someone else's mind, so get into the technologist's mind and think about how to translate your principles into something that will make sense and that they'll see value in.

While our languages might differ, technologists and designers do share some similarities, including a common trait that we regularly get tarnished with: 'focusing on the nice shiny things'. I've only heard this phrase used in relation to designers, so it was refreshing to hear Rebecca apply it to technologists:

> As technologists, we're often just so focused on the nice shiny things. We'll be talking to a VP of a business unit and trying to tell them how cool something really is, but he doesn't care about that, he cares about how it's going to support the delivery of business value.

---

* https://agilemanifesto.org/principles.html

Technologists, I think, implicitly now understand that we're not great at having customer empathy, which is necessary to design a really compelling product. But we want to understand how you do it, and so I think that's the first thing to focus on if you're coming into a tech organisation. Try to meet the technologists where they are. We're problem solvers, we're not hostile to design. We're hostile to potentially superficial reality, and there are some designers who are all flash and no substance.

Designers need to demonstrate that there's real substance. They have the techniques and approaches to get to the substance of the problem and know how somebody is going to respond to a product and how you can make that response more positive. As technologists, we want that, but we don't always understand how you do it or how we can support you in doing it.

I know it sounds like I'm putting all of the responsibility on the designers, and I'm not, because it's up to us to meet you where you are as well. But if the dominant culture is the tech culture, it's going to have to be the designers who make the first move.

As designers we need to approach working for a tech consultancy or tech company the same as we would with any customer problem we're solving or product we're creating— we need to get into the heads of the developers, empathise with them and bring them along on the journey. If developers fall into the trap of focusing on the nice shiny bit of tech, help them communicate what that really means in the language of the business and how it enhances the customer's experience.

Being empathetic and getting into the heads of our customers, users and those we work with to help us gather all the data points enables us to create a compelling story that will resonate with the recipient and be in their language—and that will help us climb the ladder and become design leaders, not only inside a tech organisation, but any organisation. This is where having emotional intelligence will help the design leaders of the future. We need to use our natural traits of empathy, curiosity and creativity to fashion our stories and clearly articulate value at increasing levels in the organisation.

You need people to walk away feeling something at the end of your presentation, and people remember stories. Stories are inherently personal and relatable and enable you to make connections that are meaningful to the audience. That might be why, according to analysis by Carmine Galo in Forbes,[*] 65–72% of the most successful TED talks are made up of stories that connect with the audience on a deeply emotional level.

Rebecca feels that creating different versions of the same story to get buy-in and bring different people on board with your idea and vision is a big part of climbing the ladder, especially in a tech consultancy:

---

[*] https://www.forbes.com/sites/carminegallo/2014/02/25/ted-talks-are-wildly-addictive-for-threepowerful-scientific-reasons/?sh=355118456b6a

A designer coming in at a consultant or senior level, for example, would be expected to be able to convey ideas and demonstrate their value to the team. Then you become a lead designer, so now you've got to talk to the tech leads and architects; then to get to a principal you have to be able to articulate the overall value of what you're doing with your specialisation lens to a chief product officer, a chief data officer or a CEO. At each level it requires getting more detailed and more specific about the outcome.

So I think about why a CEO would want to talk to me—what value am I bringing to this conversation? What can I tell them about their business, what can I tell them about the problems their customers are facing and how we might address those problems? The higher up you get, the more it matters how you communicate and what you communicate.

And that's what so many technologists also fall down on. You can talk about the bright shiny technology things to a CTO, but a CEO is not going to care about those things; they care about what they're going to achieve and want a credible story of how you can help them realise that outcome. That means changing the terms that you're using to map your audience. That's the big thing that changes as you go up the ladder: who you're talking to and what they care about. It's the same story, just told in different ways to different audiences.

Rebecca is highly respected for her technical expertise and has seen

> **"Helping technologists understand how design can result in better technology will give designers that seat at the table."**

Thoughtworks change from a purely technical company to one that takes a human-centred approach. And rather than bolting on design as an afterthought, the company has experimented through co-creation to embody strategy, design and technology. We talked about what advice she would give to designers, based on the huge changes she has seen over the years.

I take it as a given that in a number of years most companies will be technology companies that happen to do something. But that doesn't mean technologists are going to rule the world, because we can't, we can't do it in isolation.

I think helping technologists understand how design can result in better technology will give designers that seat at the table for all of the technological advances that are going to be happening. Because technology and design, sitting as separate things, just doesn't make sense.

And the way the world is going, if you stay in the game, then you'll have that seat at the table on all of the wonderful things that are going to be created, and you're going to help make them even more wonderful by saying, 'Oh, by the way, did you think about this, this thing over there that you're ignoring?'

And so I think design has the ability to significantly influence the path that the technological advances take. But that's going to require designers and technologists to work together, not each of us sitting in our own little silo sniping at each other.

"Because technology and design, sitting as separate things, just doesn't make sense."

Influencing and leading in a remote world

While some organisations, such as InVision®, have built their entire business around remote working, many have feared it, thinking it 'won't work for them' or productivity will be lost. Before COVID-19, Adam Grant, a social scientist, best-selling author and professor at the Wharton School of Business, spoke to three leaders of the biggest and most forward-thinking companies in Silicon Valley. He wanted to understand if they would ever consider allowing staff to work from home one day a week. He was shocked at the response—they all said they would never do that because it's not how they work.

Then the pandemic threw organisations into a state of panic, as they had to pivot very quickly to enable people to work remotely. We also saw a surge in companies' suddenly needing to up their digital game and realising how far behind they actually were when it came to creating engaging or even functional user experiences. Adam says what is interesting is that the three companies he interviewed have completely changed their minds since the pandemic, announcing they will probably never go back to the old ways. This is something that has been reflected by many other companies; they now realise that a huge number of people can work from anywhere, albeit some will always have to be in the physical location.

So, how does this change how we need to lead? Can we still be effective working remotely—or can we even be more effective? A lot of consultants have said that not much has changed for them because they are well accustomed to working both remotely and in person. I asked design consultants across the globe if they had noticed particular approaches that successful leaders were taking with influencing remotely that the rest of us could also use:

- **Growing their leadership by growing others.** I have seen senior people turn off their cameras when others are struggling to be heard and seen. Doing this can give space to others on the team to be more outspoken.

- **Remote first actually means more touchpoints, not fewer.** The myth is that we can take our old ways of working and add Zoom® and MURAL® and everything will work out. Those leaders who already focus on transparency have had to amplify that. They are the ones who understand that remote first actually means more touchpoints, not fewer. The team needs visibility into the system in ways they never have had before. Being the facilitator to online collaboration, whether synchronous or asynchronous, takes effort to keep people engaged, ideas flowing and decisions being made.

- **Showing up.** A lot of success comes from just showing up, and for a remote world that means showing up on a Zoom call.

- **Collaborate to align.** It's tempting when working remotely to think things through on your own and stay siloed. It's good to digest and synthesise on your own at times, but make sure you take that extra step to continue to collaborate, as understanding can get lost so quickly when we're working separately.

- **More confidence.** Not having to deal with an entire room looking at you when you're speaking or worrying about your body language can give you more confidence to speak up.

- **Getting your voice heard.** Online meetings and workshops can also make it hard for some people to get their voice heard or judge the right moments to ask a question or make a point. Setting the expected etiquette at the start of the meeting, as you would with any face-to-face meeting, helps—for instance, telling people when you would like them to ask questions, asking people to write any questions in the chat or showing them how to use the 'raised hand' tool. Many of these are now standard practice, and people naturally start using them without asking. As a design consultant, you will always be dealing with a variety of clients and customers with different levels of technology knowledge, so explaining how you want people to behave in the meeting will enable more people to have a voice.

When it comes to getting your point across, Jennifer Martin says she practises what she is going to say over and over to make sure it has the right emphasis, and you can still do this before remote meetings. Remote also enables you to have your notes clearly in front of you—the people on the other side can't see you're being prompted from your screen—and this can help you come across as being much more natural. Andy says, 'A lot of the pathway into leadership is sort of gift of the gab and being able to improvise and wing it while sounding like you know what you're talking about. The good thing about working remotely, if you're someone who is nervous speaking 'off the cuff', is that you are able to have these "invisible" notes and prompts'.

Having notes also helps you bring people back to the structure that you want to take them through in any kind of meeting or workshop and can help prevent the 'deer in the headlights' situation. However, Andy points out the downside of remote meetings:

> It is very unnatural to be staring someone in the face with a little mirror of you over their shoulder for a long time. It's also very easy, just because of technology and the way audio mixing works, for someone to dominate the conversation over the top of other people. It can be tougher to be more assertive.

- **Reading the room.** It can be hard to read the room remotely; it's much easier to pick up on body language when everyone's in a room together, especially when you're presenting. For online client presentations, especially showcases, it's a good idea to get members of your team to 'pin' the views of specific stakeholders and monitor their reactions. You can then discuss these as a team after the meeting. Sounds a bit creepy, but body language and the language people use can give away a lot.

- **Team uplift.** If you're not using a special usability testing room with a one-way mirror—and let's face it, not many people have access to that!—it can be difficult to have multiple people observing. As designers, we don't want to make customers feel intimidated by having too many pairs of eyes on them or running the risk of too many people asking questions; but as design consultants, we also want to educate our clients by bringing them along on the journey and motivate our team to be more human centred by involving them in research and testing.

Conducting usability testing remotely enables you to have extra people joining the sessions; they simply sit on the call with their cameras off. This approach has meant I've been able to uplift more people across a client's organisation—from marketing teams, design teams, product managers and developers—within a few days. Showing value as quickly as possible and bringing more people along on the journey helps you spread your influence across more areas of the business more quickly and gets your name out there.

- **Easier to access customers.** The advantage of more people working from home when conducting usability testing has made it far easier to test with users in both regional and metro areas. We're no longer needing to travel to them, or they to us, and it also gives extra insight into where they live, which sometimes is missed. Response times when asking for users is far quicker, and being able to tap into customers more easily enables you to add value more quickly. The reduced overheads and ease of access to users is also a bonus for clients and reduces some of the resistance when trying to get sign-off for usability testing.

Delegate to increase your leadership

The journey to leadership is a team effort—it's those around you who help you get to where you want to be and achieve more. We designers tend to have lots of ideas and solutions to problems, but we can't achieve everything alone, so you need to encourage and inspire those around you to help research and experiment with new ideas. It doesn't have to be other designers helping you out; look around and see what talent and relationships you have access to and use these to help you get more done. It's also important to make sure those who help you receive the praise and recognition they deserve—nobody likes people who take the credit for their colleagues' ideas and work!

DesignedUp leaders delegate to others who are perfectly capable and enables them to achieve more and get the ideas out of their head and out into the world. While I'm a perfectionist and love seeing ideas through to fruition, I also love helping others think bigger and make their own ideas a reality—or even just encouraging them to tell their story. Helping others rise up is leadership, and those around you will have different networks helping you spread the importance of design further and more quickly while also helping them to become leaders.

I was leading a project for a major e-commerce retailer, and we needed some extra help to document and tag everything in DoveTail®. A few weeks prior, I had been chatting with one of our new graduate BAs who had just finished at Thoughtworks University

(TWU), an intensive programme that we put all our grads through. I knew she was keen to 'shadow' on a project and get stuck in, so I asked if we could bring her into the project to help her see how things really work with a client.

She was fantastic and went from knowing nothing about DoveTail or how design really works to mastering the tool by pairing with our researcher, helping to undertake research and gaining a deep knowledge of the customers. I encouraged her to present some of the findings in our showcase and to run a training session with the client's designers on how they could maximise their DoveTail account, extract more details and have better documentation. She won, the client won and I won—both personally and professionally.

Sometimes you will have ideas that will help solve a problem and expand design across an organisation, and you pull the relevant people into the conversation and try to drive the idea as you have in the past. Then conversations happen in the background and suddenly someone you pulled into the conversation turns it into something they are then driving. While you are still part of the team, you're not leading, and they appear to be taking all the glory. Yes, this has happened to me, and although it hurts, you have to rise above it and think about the bigger picture. At the end of the day, it's not about who's steering the ship, it's about whether it's going to solve the problem, benefit the company and help scale design.

Erica had someone hijack one of her ideas at a previous company and quickly learnt how execs can use other peoples' ideas to shoehorn their own agendas. But it also helped her realise that you can't have and own every idea. The more ideas you come up with, the better, and you might run with them yourself, share them, give them away, file them until it's the right time to bring them out—and, yes, sometimes they'll be stolen.

> Sometimes I come up with so much stuff, I will just toss it at people. They come to me with a problem and I take that idea out of the filing cabinet in my head—'I had this idea six months ago, what do you think?' If they like it, I just let them run with it, then they get credit for getting it done. I actually don't really care who gets the credit, because I'm going to know that it got out there into the world. Don't treat your ideas like gold or be precious about them, and don't be afraid to let somebody else take your idea and run with it, because it's not doing any good sitting in your head.

Where to find support

Design leaders need to seek advocates for design across all levels of the organisation or client. First and foremost, focusing inwards on the digital delivery team or design team is a good way to adopt the strategy of 'top-skill mentorship'. From this, you can grow design with those closest to you, which will then emanate out.

You will need different strategies depending on how your team is set up. If your team has multiple design archetypes—each with critical skills such as visual design, information architecture, interaction design and research or product strategy—there is a risk that one of the designers could become a bottleneck for any work that requires a particular critical skill. It's therefore important to grow the skills initially across the designers, and if the designers sit within the delivery team, to then grow the relevant skills across the remaining team.

Some skills can't easily be picked up—or should never be picked up—by other team members, such as visual design or specialist areas of research. However, training others to conduct basic usability testing or help with note-taking during testing and research sessions and then help analyse the results will reduce the load on individual researchers or designers and will, in turn, spread customer insights and empathy across the team. The aim isn't to turn non-designers into designers but to get the team to experience first-hand what the customer experiences when using the product or service and to help you gather information and insights more quickly.

Having designers pair with developers allows you to grow knowledge across the team and learn more about the technical landscape yourself. Having the specialists become mentors for those who want to grow particular design capabilities is another way to grow the knowledge, and this also starts the growth off in the right direction from the beginning. It also makes the job of the mentor easier, as they have a mentee who is actually interested in learning their skill.

Although growing the critical skills across your team may initially slow the team down, it will only be for a short while, and the whole team will quickly reap the benefits, as there will be more resources available. If the specialist on the team is tied up with other work, perhaps the newly-skilled co-worker can step in and move the project forward. Not every team is set up for mentorship—in some organisations, work is highly siloed, and some individuals aren't open to learning new skills—so this approach won't be as effective in those situations until the team becomes more open to cross-skill pollination.

If you work for a tech consultancy that typically staffs one designer per product delivery team, your approach will be very different. Your skills will also need to be different—you will have a particular archetype that is more dominant but will also have two or more other archetypes under your belt—what's referred to as being 'T-shaped'. On top of this, you will also have consulting and stakeholder management skills along with several others.

This type of team structure is at higher risk of design bottlenecks, so it's even more important to quickly up-skill others—not with specific design skills as in the previous approach, but with skills that can aid the work you're doing. This can be working closely with developers and QAs to help train their design eye for UI inconsistencies, thinking about interactions from the user's perspective; or it could be working closely with the BAs so you both have an understanding of how something will function. In your absence, the BA can easily explain the expectation of the design.

Getting everyone on the team to understand the customers will, over time, reduce the need to keep reminding people why you have designed something one way and not another. Working closely with the tech lead enables you to put practices in place to make the flow between design and tech work better and call out when something isn't working properly, then find and test a solution.

For example, I was working with a team, and all the story cards that had a design element had a brief description for the design and links to the Adobe XD file that had the flow for the particular scenario, with access to the developer view. During kick-off, we would walk through the card and design, which also had extra notes to help the developers.

We thought we'd covered everything, but we still had issues with the developers' missing really important items from the designs. When I asked the developers if they had read my design notes—and if not, would they prefer I did something different—they were all too polite to say no. I later found out that actually some of them weren't reading my notes—this embarrassingly came up on a desk check. We all laughed about it; they were young developers, and I think they felt a bit intimidated by me.

To help solve this issue, I gave the team some options I'd used in the past that had worked and asked for their opinions on how we could make things work better for them. The tech lead, iteration manager and I discussed the problem and introduced the following:

Because the developers only looked at the acceptance criteria, I placed a large table in the Jira card (see Figure 6.2) under the Acceptance Criteria header, called Design. It had two columns: Description/Interaction/Design and Done. The developers could then place a tick in the Done column for each design item. The Description column would also have the link to the design file and would clearly say how many screens or pages were in the prototype, as they often missed this detail at the bottom of the screen. It then went on to list specific details they had missed in the past.

After stand-up each morning, we held a design catch-up where the developers could show me the progress on the design and ask any questions. This helped immensely, as I was only part-time on the project and not always around for kick-offs. We also held pre-desk checks to ensure everything worked well before we showed the product owner.

This all added to the design overhead, and there was a risk that it would really slow the process of getting cards ready for development, but it was needed. We saw a huge improvement very quickly, and it greatly reduced the need for re-work.

Every team you work in will have different levels of experience, and the more experience you have, the more scenarios and solutions you will be familiar with to mitigate problems. With all the best intentions, you may start with an approach that has worked before, and for some reason it won't work with your new team. You'll need to adapt, which is where having advocates for design will help you greatly with your cause.

Description/Interaction/Design	Done
Here's the link to the design/prototype: https:// . . . Please do the following to see the developer view . . .	
Here's the link to the styleguide: https:// . . .	
Lydia (persona name) would like to be able to do . . . Why does Lydia want to be able to do this? . . .	
We are doing . . .	
The interaction is expected to behave like https:// . . .	
The accessibility requirements are . . .	

Figure 6.2 Example of design table in Jira. However, as design software and Jira or similar evolve, this will change; for example, at the time of writing, Jira had a plugin for Figma files.

Where are the best places to find advocates?

After you've established the advocates for design within your team, you need to start growing your advocates outside the team and across the organisation. Naturally, designers have much in common with marketing and customer-care teams. They are both in tune with the customers and are a great resource for gathering branding styles, customer insights and data, which you can later use to measure the success of the products or services you are building.

I also find these teams are usually the ones siloed away from digital products or the IT teams, yet they are needed to bring insights into the product, help with marketing and offer customer support once it's out in the wild. You will find they are usually very willing to help.

During workshops with executives and sponsors, listen to those who talk about the customer or business problem they want to solve. Ask yourself if those problems can be solved with design and how you might demonstrate that. During one showcase I did, an exec made a side comment on the styleguide I'd put in place to speed up design and delivery and ensure we created a consistent product. He mentioned that, to make all their products consistent and faster to design, it would be useful to have all their teams work with what I'd put in place. I followed this up in a later conversation with him and offered to show his team what we were doing, which led to my attending their technical council meeting, where I presented on the value in continuous usability testing, the time it saves having a consistent style and how it positively impacts the customer and brand experience.

You need to find who in the organisation feels the most repercussions from customers' poor experience of the product or service—such as the technical or product support team, who have to answer the same questions and walk customers through the same problems time after time, simply because something isn't worded clearly or the interface is confusing.

Some research we were conducting for a legacy system uncovered that one of the most frequent calls the customer-care team had was regarding connecting the printer to the software they were using. Solving this problem for the customer would also help reduce the number of calls, freeing up staff time to serve customers with larger problems.

It may be that the sales team are struggling to sell a product because it's hard to demonstrate its value and the problem it solves. Or the finance team might have to create lengthy workarounds to take customer payments, which results in the customer's thinking a payment hasn't gone through and paying twice, meaning more work for the finance team to correct it.

Linking the customers' frustrations with the employees' frustrations across the organisation, both inside and outside of your delivery team, will help you create a compelling story to solve customer and employee problems and strengthen the value design gives. If you can link these to the work your delivery team are doing, it will enable you to share how the experiences you are creating and problems you are solving ripple out across the organisation. For many designers, especially those who specialise in service design, this will be a no-brainer. Working as a consultant across multiple organisations and teams, you'll find many of the problems are similar, but how you tackle them will need to be different.

Teams are busy working in their own worlds, focusing on getting their jobs done and creating workarounds to solve problems without realising that some of their pains could easily be fixed. Or they may have raised an issue but it's not been addressed because the people who could fix it have other priorities. Being the person who connects the dots, has empathy for these other teams and can identify how both customer and employee problems can be solved will help you spread the value of design and find support.

There is always a team leader who is not only managing the team but also monitoring their performance to make them more efficient—reduce support costs, reduce support calls, ensure production is more efficient and increase sales. Finding these people usually isn't very hard, and they are generally very receptive to helping because they also want happy customers and happy employees.

Some of these people may not know that the root cause of their issue is user experience, or they may have thought it couldn't be solved or even been told it was too hard to fix. Getting these people on board can result in a variety of positive outcomes, including helping you gather customer insights and data, finding new people to help with usability testing and interviews, growing the knowledge of design, finding support for design, and adding more value to the organisation, the customer and the employees. Also, each of these leaders will have different connections within the business, different levels of influence and different budgets. This will help you get more support for design and potentially budget from other areas to solve some of their issues, rather than it always falling on product/delivery/IT teams.

Advocates for customer and employee experience are everywhere in an organisation. We need to seek them out and show that their experience can be improved and problems solved through the use of design.

So, in summary . . .

No matter your level of experience as a designer, there is always something to learn and improve on when it comes to how you influence.

Many people within organisations, at all levels, don't fully understand what design is or the impact it has, and it's our job to teach them. In doing that, we need to take others along on the design journey, showing where design adds value and why we do the things we do. That could be getting your team involved in usability testing to gain more empathy for the customer and reduce the questions around why you designed the solution the way you did. It could be taking the execs out to meet customers so they can experience the real-world user experience for themselves and better understand the problems we uncover and the solutions we put forward.

It's also our job to pay attention to the needs and fears of the execs. What will the people we're working with lose if it all goes wrong? The more we can understand and have empathy for the decision-makers, the better we'll be able to tailor our storytelling and the more effectively we'll be able to influence them so we achieve the best outcomes for our clients, our customers, our teams and the business.

Design leaders are the glue that melds the customer, design, tech, data and business into a compelling story that is human at its core.

As you bring others along on the design journey, take the time and care to be understanding, helpful and empathetic. Demonstrate passion for your work and for the vision, and be true to yourself—that's how you'll build a tribe of followers who will advocate for you and help broaden your sphere of influence.

But remember, as a leader it's not just about influencing up, it's also about being humble and showing appreciation to those who have supported you. A simple thank you goes a long way.

Oh, and while you're on your path to design leadership, don't be afraid to go rogue!

———————————

sev

one final note

A story is not complete without an ending, something that summarises not only the journey, but also the facts; what has been learnt and where to go next. But it should also leave you feeling inspired and ready to challenge the status quo—for if we do not challenge, everything will stay the same.

eing DesignedUp falls into two areas: DesignedUp organisations and DesignedUp design leaders. However, the former cannot happen without the latter, nor can it be achieved through acquiring design agency after design agency and hoping the worlds of business and technology will magically be transformed so they're driven by design.

DesignedUp leaders are not made through simply taking a few design thinking courses and talking the talk, nor is it about honing your design craft until you're 100% perfect—no one is perfect. It's about being good at your craft, educating those around you about the advantages design brings, taking people along on the journey to understand what design is, building tribes—and doing it all while staying true to who you are and being an all-round nice human.

I'm hopeful that more and more people in the industry will start to be exposed to these very competent designers, especially in UX, and begin to appreciate the better results you can get at the end of the day when you've got those specialists on your team.

Mike Mason, Global Head of Technology,
Office of the CTO, Thoughtworks®

Opportunity

We've been in a unique position for the last few years, where we've had the opportunity to shape the experiences being created by technology and business consultancies and organisations. This opportunity is growing thanks to the demands of users and the drive for advances in technology, for better and faster experiences and for consultancies and organisations either acquiring design agencies or growing their own design capability organically.

And while 'design thinking' has been misinterpreted by many and is now in danger of damaging design and its value through over-commercialisation, it started a much-needed conversation and broke down the complexities and nuances of design in a way businesses driven by process could understand. However, DesignedUp leaders still need to prove to their stakeholders, who are treating it as a 'tick box' exercise, to unpack how it really works—the value design brings, especially in a cross-functional team—and introduce them to the full breadth of design, from research, service design, interaction, visual, designOps and beyond.

Designers working in tech companies have the opportunity to shape how design works and take non-designers along on the journey to embrace what design can bring. Maybe a few can be converted to join us and help the clients we work with solve their problems and achieve their vision through employing design rather than simply throwing more developers at the problem. In tech and business consultancies, designers can influence the value design brings within the consultancy and for every client. And DesignedUp consultants have the opportunity to impact not just one organisation but many, and this means positively impacting millions of humans— customers, consultants and employees alike.

Finding advocates and understanding and allaying the fears of executives enables us to curate conversations that resonate and effectively articulate how design works, solves the right problem and brings value. And that's how we garner influence.

Learn and evolve

Understanding and playing to your strengths will help you hone them. But, like any good design problem, what works for one audience or team may not work for another, so you will need to experiment with your approaches and build a toolkit that can handle any situation.

DesignedUp leaders need to learn from the past and be the best version of themselves —not another 'hand waver' without substance, or that narcissistic, arrogant type who puts other designers down due to their own lack of underlying confidence and internal imposter syndrome. Designers need to work with others across the organisation to solve the problems of today and tomorrow, bring others along on the journey and grow their tribes. We need to translate design into the tech and business languages that others speak, because we are in 'their world', and it's our responsibility to make ourselves understood.

DesignedUp leaders lead with kindness, authenticity and without apology. Find mentors and role models to learn from, both inside and outside of design, and always challenge and seek to understand those who are blocking your career progression. Don't take sh*t from the 1%—either shut them down with evidence or just move on. They're not worth the wasted oxygen.

Others are doing it—so can you

There are designers working within tech companies and consultancies who are changing the conversation and are influencing all the way to the top. And there are clients who are at various stages of transformation who are listening to DesignedUp leaders to enable them to become better themselves and create better experiences for their customers.

There are design leaders like Shelley Evenson, who embraced the acquisition of Fjord as an opportunity to take their ideas of how things could be all the way through to implementation. There are design leaders who are committed to avoiding the mistakes made by others when their design agencies have been acquired. There are the teams who have grown organically through recognising the need for design, such as Thoughtworks, continually adjusting and working together as one to become something better.

No matter where you are on your journey, I invite you to use the stories and ideas in this book to help you take the next step in your leadership journey. And if you're not being given the space to grow or the opportunities you want, it might be time to make a change and find a new environment where you can flourish.

Lead the way

Leaders are not assigned their role; they emerge out of a passion for being and wanting more. They have a tribe, they find advocates for design in order to influence, they help executives overcome their fears and achieve their vision. They continually strive to make the world of tomorrow better than the world today, to improve the experience of everything we touch and enable teams and stakeholders to trust in the design approach.

The tech and consulting world can be hard and frustrating at times. Continually explaining the value of design and how it really works to clients, stakeholders and the teams we work with can be tiring and often feel like 'Groundhog Day'. It's repetitive, and with every new team and client the narrative will need adjusting. But to have impact and take those around us on the journey, we need to be prepared to make the first move.

As a design leader, you have to be willing and able to speak up, not only for yourself but also for others. Call out bad behaviour whenever you see it and don't let gender come into the equation. If you want to lead, then lead, and if you have your eyes set on a particular mentor, just ask them – what have you got to lose? Only seven percent of women negotiate their first salary, compared to fifty-seven percent of men. Let's change that ratio, challenge the status quo and start saying 'yes' a lot more.

What's next

I hope this book has inspired you to say 'yes' more and embrace the unknown. It's okay not to be 100% sure and to make it up as you go long. Leadership isn't about knowing what to do, it's about embracing the ambiguity and making what you feel is the best decision at the time with the information you have. No matter where you are on your path, take one or two of the stories, methods or approaches in this book to make a change—and if one approach doesn't work, try a different one and see what resonates. But, whatever you do, stay true to who you are, become the best version of yourself and carry your core skills and strengths with you, always.

Once you're a DesignedUp leader, you can then spread and scale your influence and help the organisations, consultancies and clients you work for and with become DesignedUp—driven by design, rather than driving design.

I'd love to hear about your journey and what has or hasn't worked, so feel free to connect with me on LinkedIn and tell me your story.

Andreas Markdalen, Global Chief Creative Officer at frog, gives these words of advice:

> **Be the leader you never had. Every step in the journey has its own benefits and its own challenges, but by staying true to yourself, staying true to your core values; being curious, authentic and always trying to push yourself to expand your reach into new areas, you can forge your own path and make your mark in a way that is true and unique to you.**
>
> **I've been fortunate to have been surrounded by leaders I respect and admire through most of my career. I've always reflected on why I'm drawn to certain people and what characteristics inspire me in a mentor or collaborator. I try to model myself around those while bringing my own ideas into the mix. It's a life-long journey, and the work to improve never ends.**
>
> **My message to young designers is to seek a leadership growth path that is right for them over time. Don't rush it too much, and let your approaches and ideas grow organically. It's not a race to the end. The best leaders manage to connect the dots between the past, the present and the future; but each leader tells their own story, in their own way. Make sure you tell your story, and that it matters to you.**

---

nk you.

just as great experiences can only be achieved through cross-functional teams, insights from customers, testing and learning, being inspired and sometimes being bold enough to take the path untrodden, is also true for writing and designing a book.

This book was created not through happenstance, but through wanting to solve a problem and help fellow designers trying to navigate the world of tech and consulting, those who want to be brave, make a difference, articulate the value they create, bring others into our world of design, make experiences of tomorrow better than they are today and avoid having their hard work de-prioritised because it is not understood.

This book wouldn't be the book it is without the help of my trusted editors Susan Culligan and Sarah Walker: thank you for making my words and ideas make sense. Susan, you allowed me to design a book I could be proud of and put my design stamp all over; I must have driven you crazy on a number of occasions with all my tweaks, but we worked as a team, bouncing ideas back

Adam Cellary Founder and CEO RealEye®

Adam Hope Principal Experience Designer, Thoughtworks®

Andreas Markdalen Global Chief Creative Officer at frog®

Ange Ferguson Chief Transformation Officer, Thoughtworks

Dr Andy Polaine Ex Global Group Design Director of Client Evolution at Fjord®

Brian Henesey Forrester

Bronwyn Shimmin-Clarke Principal Product Manager, Thoughtworks

Caroline Teahan Australian Staffing Lead, Thoughtworks

Cassandra Kelsall Director of Experience at Publicis Sapient

Catriona Burgess Head of Frost Place, part of Frost*collective

Claire Nelson Lead Experience Designer, Thoughtworks

Darren Smith Chief Product & Technology Officer, MYOB

Diana Adorno Principal Product & Behavioural Scientist, Thoughtworks

Edwina Fox Marketing specialist, UAP®

Erica Rider DesignOps Leader at PayPal®

Evan Bottcher Head of Architecture, MYOB

Fiona Byarugaba Employer Brand Manager & DEI Lead, Thoughtworks

Gareth Morgan Global Head of Marketing & Content, Thoughtworks

Gilbert Guaring Head of Marketing & Communications, UAP

Heidi Munc VP of UX, Nationwide®

Helen Barlow-Hunt Finance Director, Australia, Thoughtworks

Ian Cartwright Tech Director, UK, Thoughtworks

Ian Kelsall Principal of Product Management, Australia, Thoughtworks

Jaksha Shah Lead Business Analyst, Thoughtworks

Jean Zheng Director of Legal, Australia, Thoughtworks

Jeff Gothelf Author, *Lean UX* and *Sense & Respond*

Jennifer Martin Associate Partner, AsiaPacific Experience Design Leader, EY

John Maeda VP of Design & Artificial Intelligence, Microsoft®

John Wyzalek Senior Acqusitions Editor, Taylor & Francis Group®

JoJo Swords Content Lead, Global Customer Marketing, Thoughtworks

Joshua Kinal Lead Experience Designer, Thoughtworks

Karen Dumville Global Head of Marketing Operations, Thoughtworks

Kate Linton Head of Design, Thoughtworks

Kathleen Casford Founder of By Ninja

Kavitha Thyagarajan Lead Designer, Thoughtworks

and forth across the globe. Sarah, thanks for having my back and coming to the rescue on a number of occasions.

Of course there is also my long-suffering husband, who has again been by my side as I embarked on another book. This time was much harder with two young children, careers and businesses to manage, but as always we found a way to get it to work.

But the team that made this possible is much larger than those mentioned above. And while I originally planned to write you all a personal note of thanks, I have unfortunately run out of my page allowance; however, I have just enough space to include all your names. Thank you team for your valued consult and support—without you this book would not have been possible:

- All the clients I have ever worked with apart from the not-to-be-named 1%-ers.

- All those who cannot be mentioned—your input was invaluable.

- And for any that I may have missed, it's not intentional—I've just spoken to so many wonderful humans during the creation of this book.

Kevin Yeung Head of Data Platform at 3P Learning

Kit Rion Citation Specialist, Forrester

Kristan Vingrys Managing Director, APAC, Thoughtworks

Lauren Pleydell-Pearce Executive Creative Director, PWC® UK

Liz Gilleran Senior Experience Designer, Thoughtworks

Luciana Albuquerque Gissing Creative Director, Experience Design at Deloitte® Digital in LA.

Maria Gomez Director of Engineering at BCG Digital Ventures®, Berlin

Mariel Maciá Senior Service Design Manager, McKinsey & Company®

Mark Carter Long-suffering husband

Mark Collin Head of Retail, Europe, Thoughtworks

Mark Togher Head of Professional Services, Australia, Thoughtworks

Martin Fowler Chief Scientist, Thoughtworks

Matthew Johnston Head of Disability Inclusion, Thoughtworks

Matthew Haynes Founder, The Design Conference, Brisbane, Australia

Matthew Tobin Founder & Managing Director, UAP

Mike Mason Global Head of Technology, Thoughtworks

Natalie Day Head of Marketing, Australia, Thoughtworks

Neal Ford Software Architect Director, Author, Thoughtworks

Nic Smyth Director or Customer Experience Product & Design, Australia, Thoughtworks

Nina Merriam Solution Specialist, Reprints, Forrester

Rebecca Parsons Chief Technology Officer, Thoughtworks

Reyne Quackenbush Global Head of Analyst Relations, Thoughtworks

Ryan Rumsey CEO and Founder at Second Wave Dive and former Assistant Vice President of Experience Strategy at USAA®

Sara Michelazzo Director of Strategy & Change, Customer Experience, Thoughtworks

Sarah Taraporewalla Director of Enterprise Modernisation, Platforms and Cloud, Thoughtworks

Sarah Walker Editor

Sofia Woods Product Design Director at Xero

Susan Culligan Production Coordinator, DerryField Publishing Services

Swapnil Deshpande Chief Digital Officer, Thoughtworks

The Thoughtworks design community

Theron Shreve Director, Derryfield Publishing Services

Tiago Griffo Head of Strategy, Thoughtworks

Tony Smith Client Engagement Partner, Fujitsu®

Tiago Duate Engagement Manager, Amazon Web Services®